Penny

Powerful Beginner's Guide to Dominate Stocks

by

Jordon Sykes

are for clarifying purposes only and are the owned by the owners themselves, not affiliated with this document.

Table Of Contents

Part-III

Introduction

I want to thank you and congratulate you for buying the book, "Penny Stocks".

This book contains proven steps and strategies on how to learn about what penny stocks are, the concepts behind them, and how to figure out whether they are right for you to get interested in. Trading and investing are tempting subjects for anyone who wants to be free from the concerns of money, and who doesn't?

What if you found out that on the screen that is right in front of you right now, you had all of the tools needed to change your life for the better? It's true. We are living in a very exciting time that gives anyone with an internet connection and the ability to read a chance at making a better life for themselves.

By the end of this book, I hope you will feel much better versed in the world of penny stocks and feel ready to make a decision about whether or not to pursue this path further or not.

This is not an easy path to go down, and it takes time, effort, and patience, but where you are now is a great place to start. Learning about this subject will be challenging at times, but it's the type of challenge that just about anyone can live up to if they only have the right information and attitude. In this book, you will find that we review certain definitions or risks multiple times. This is because just starting out in stocks can be confusing and overwhelming, and the goal is to get the most important ideas through so you can make an informed choice about getting involved in them.

Thanks again for buying this book, I hope you enjoy it!

Chapter 1: Penny Stock Basics

Everyone is tempted by ideas of getting rich quick, and anyone who has researched stocks even for a few minutes knows about these temptations well. The internet is full of empty promises of early retirement, making a million dollars in a week, or more. The reality of the situation is that getting rich quick does happen to a rare few, but this is not a common occurrence. IPOs and penny stocks are tempting to many people and for some, can be a great choice for an investment, but your average, every day investor doesn't have the skill or the time to research these investments thoroughly enough to make it worth the effort.

Before you decide to get involved in this world, it's a good idea to decide if it's right for you. Starting with this guide is a great beginning. Let's cover some of the most basic information about penny stocks so you can make an informed decision.

Penny Shares or Penny Stocks:

Penny shares or penny stocks refer to stocks that trade, usually, below $5 in the United States, or below £3 in Europe. Typically, these equities don't trade within markets of major standing, for example the New York Stock Exchange or the London Stock Exchange. Rather, these equities go through less structured, smaller exchanges. In the United Kingdom, these may be traded using the OFEX (or the Off Exchange), or the AIM (or the Alternative Investment Market). The version in the United States that is comparable to this is called the OTCBB (or the Over the Counter Bulletin Board). Alternatively, something called Pink Sheets is also used, which refers to a quote system getting published for stocks that occur over the counter.

Trading Penny Stocks can be a Risky Game:

Penny shares arc known as risky, and there are a few different reasons why this is so. In this section, we will review the more pressing of these reasons.

1. Less Information to Base Trades Off of: One major factor for shares trading at very low prices is that the business itself is either unprofitable, or has not yet established for itself a good financially stable track record.

Solid, trustworthy and reliable companies that have a supporting and strong history of finances don't typically need to resort to over the counter trades. Usually, these companies will be associated with the main exchange instead.

2. Listing Requirements for these Stocks are not as Strict as Others: An issue with trying to research businesses that deal over the counter is the issue of requirements for listing being far less stringent than they are with bigger exchanges. This makes it harder to receive a reliable gauge of the financial fortitude of the company or its future potential.

This can lead investors to feel as though they are gambling or guessing with their investments, and no one likes that feeling. When it comes to our hard-earned cash, we want as much security as possible. For this reason, anyone starting out in penny stocks should only do so with capital that they don't need.

3. Penny Stocks can Lose Overnight Considerably: Penny stocks are obviously priced quite low, which can lead to troublesome situations for certain investors. When prices go down to 50 cents or even lower, someone can buy hundreds of shares, or even thousands, quite easily, hoping that the shares will go up in value fast. It's easy to rationalize that if a stock costs only a few cents, it only has to rise a few more to make a profit.

But the issues can multiply in this situation. If someone doesn't do enough research, shares can be likely to go down a few cents as they are to raise a few cents. Another issue is a plan for exiting a trade. A lot of investors who are not yet experienced don't bother to prepare a quality plan for exiting, or don't have the discipline to execute their pre-conceived plans. Penny stocks can change quickly and are known as volatile, which means that yes, they can go up a lot in just a couple of days. However, if you're not fast enough with selling or find that you cannot sell, they can fall quite fast, as well.

4. Problems with Liquidity: A factor that plays a role in the volatility of penny stocks is their liquidity. Since there are not unlimited amounts of people investing in or trading penny stocks on average, getting rid of shares precisely when you decide to may be harder than you think. To sell something at a chosen price, you have to be able to locate someone who is willing to purchase it.

Being unable to find someone to buy could result in a forced lowering of the price, which could decrease profits for you immediately (if you were previously in a position that was profitable). Similar to that, if you decide to sell because you see that shares are going down in price, you run the risk of prices collapsing if prospective buyers don't want to purchase at the price you are hoping for.

Information on IPOs (or Initial Public Offerings):

Big companies, sometimes, make the choice to make their information public, listing their share information on a major platform. Before doing this, the company files for an IPO, or initial public offering. When the time draws closer, the business will release its first stock price and allow investors to show interest in purchasing shares for it. These can be bought from underwriters, or the stockbrokers that work issuing IPO for the specific company. Underwriters also aid in determining appropriate prices and then do the marketing and selling of the shares for the company, raising money for the business. This is one of the harder aspects of IPO issuing and is among the factors in why they are risky, at times, for people who decide to invest.

The Way IPO Value is Determined:

During an IPO, a company's value can be decided by looking at several qualities. Underwriters utilize the financial information of the company, along with management information, information about the corporate structure, and more, to decide on a price. The other, undefined factors can be difficult to measure or pin down specifically. If the shares are priced too low by the underwriter, it means that a company may be leaving money out, since they only receive funds for shares that got sold at the same time of the IPO. As soon as shares get traded on an open exchange, they do not belong to the company and the price of them is decided, instead, by the state of the market at that time.

IPOs have Great Potential for Investing:

Although IPOs can be volatile, they can be a good choice for investing. In fact, every year there are a few excellent ones that show up in the market. But, the average person who is interested in investing typically doesn't have the resources necessary to figure out the risk and reward potentials for them. At all times, there is a quality of chance involved with IPO participation. The idea is to lower the risk as much as possible, and the only way this is possible is through plenty of research and knowledge acquired over time.

Penny Stocks and IPOs:

For some investors, the reward potential that penny stocks and IPOs offer is far too wonderful to miss out on. Some good advice for these people in terms of investing in penny shares and IPOs is that you should learn the most you can about which company you choose to invest in. Never make decisions based on emotion or bias.

Create a solid plan for entry and exit for whichever position you decide on and make sure you stick to this plan.

In addition, never commit a large amount of your portfolio to investments that are risky. While investing small amounts of money into investments that are high risk with good chances of reward can be okay with enough research and wealth; putting yourself in a position like this with a high amount of capital is extremely risky and potentially dangerous. Even people who are successful with risky financial investments should have plenty of money to rely on if things go bad. That being said, penny stocks and IPO can be highly exciting, pay off greatly, and can be fun to learn about, and eventually become part of a balanced investment portfolio.

More on Basic Penny Stock Information:

Companies that enjoy success do not happen overnight. They are made with lots of hard work and usually start from simple beginnings, moving their way up slowly, like anything else of value. Some investors, unfortunately, are operating under the belief that discovering the next huge thing translates to searching existing penny stocks to discover the next Apple. However, this strategy hardly ever works out and only happens to a rare few. If you are going into this with the hopes of discovering the next Wal-Mart in a penny stock, this may not be the best field for you.

What are Micro-cap Stocks?

The terms "micro-cap stocks" and "penny stocks" basically mean the same thing and can be used in place of each other. Micro-cap stocks are, technically, defined that way because of market capitalizations, but penny stocks have their name based on how much they cost. These definitions can vary slightly, but typically, stocks that have market capitalization above $50 million but below $300 million can be referred to as a micro-cap. If it goes below $50 million, it's called a nano-cap. As we mentioned earlier, stocks that go below $5 are penny stocks, although some consider it anything below $3, and others still under $1.

An important factor to keep in mind about penny stocks, which we have already discussed a bit in this book, is that penny stocks or micro stocks are a lot riskier than other types of stocks. We already reviewed some of those reasons earlier in this chapter, but let's review them again in different terms to make sure you fully understand them. We will also go over some other important risk factors.

Why are Penny Stocks Riskier than Other Types of Stocks?

☐ Less public information about penny stocks: The main way to be successful with developing a strategy for investing is gathering enough relevant and valuable information to make decisions that are informed and make sense. But information for micro-cap stocks is a lot harder to find than other stock information.

Companies that list themselves on pink sheets have no requirements for filing with the SEC (or the Securities and Exchange Commission), meaning that they are less scrutinized publicly. They are also less regulated and the information that can be found about these is simply not as credible. It's much easier to falsify, exaggerate, or downplay information for companies that aren't held to specific standards.

☐ A lack of minimum requirements for penny stocks: You will find that stocks on the pink sheets or OTCBB have no requirements to meet minimum standards to stay where they are, in terms of existing on the exchange. At times, that is the reason for a stock being on an exchange.

As soon as a company can't maintain its position anymore on a major exchange, it will move over to a smaller one. Although the OTCBB asks for companies to be timely with filing their documents using the SEC, this requirement doesn't exist for the pink sheets. Minimum requirements are a safety net for people who invest and also show benchmarks for certain businesses.

☐ No history information to be found for investors: A lot of the companies that are called micro-cap stocks are on the brink of bankruptcy or barely started. This means that they have a high chance of having no track records or very bad ones. Obviously, this makes it difficult to tell the potential of a stock. In addition to this, some companies might try to make their situation sound better than it really is to draw in investors.

You should watch out for ads for stocks that seem to promise fantastic payoffs in a short period of time. You should also be careful about investing in companies that appear to have a business idea that is very "out there" or seems too good to be true. In this world, if something seems too good to be true, it often is.

☐ More about liquidity: Two issues can come up when stocks don't have enough liquidity. First, you might run into not being able to sell it. With lower levels of liquidity, you may have a difficult time finding a buyer for specific stocks, meaning you'll have to bring the price down to make it more appealing to prospective buyers.

Second, lower levels of liquidity give traders some chances to mess with the prices of stocks, which can be done in a number of ways; buying huge amounts, hyping them up and then selling it once people find it appealing.

In addition to these risks posed by penny stocks, there are some scams that come along with them that are wise to watch out for. Here are some of the most popular of these scams, along with a few more risks to look out for in relation to penny stocks:

☐ Biased or false recommendations: Certain penny stock companies pay people to recommend their stocks on radio shows, finance TV or newsletters. You may find that you get spam in your e-mail inbox hyping up a certain type of stock. Any postings, recommendations, or e-mails like this should be taken with caution. Check to see if the sources of recommendations are being given money to advertise, since this gives away a bad investment. Also check to ensure that press releases aren't falsely given by individuals attempting to influence stock prices.

☐ Brokers that exist offshore: The SEC allows companies to sell their stock outside of the United States, under a certain regulation, to investors from foreign countries, to allow them to be exempt from registering those stocks. Typically, these companies will get rid of the stock at a discounted price to brokers offshore who turn around and sell them back to United States-based investors at a large profit. By gathering attractive information and cold calling, potentially interested investors off a list who have enough money to buy certain stocks, these deceitful brokers employ convincing tactics to get investors to buy their stocks.

☐ The first main fallacy of penny stocks: There are two fallacies about penny stocks that are common to investors. The first is that a lot of stocks that exist today used to be penny stocks. People who fall into this trap are under the impression that companies like Microsoft, Apple, or other huge companies started out as penny stocks that have gradually grown in value.

People make this mistaken assumption because they look at adjusted stock prices, which look at all of the stock splits. When you take a look at Microsoft or Apple, you can see that their first day trading prices were in the neighborhood of $20. These companies didn't start at a low price on the market. Actually, they started quite high and rose until the necessity to split came up.

☐ The second main fallacy of penny stocks: The second common fallacy is that the more stocks you buy, the more you make on your returns. They believe that there is more opportunity to own a lot of stock and a lot more room for the values to grow with penny stocks. If you own a stock that is worth 10 cents and it goes up by five, you have just made a 50% profit. Considering this, in combination with $1,000 investments being able to purchase 10,000 shares of stock, makes investors believe that these micro-cap stocks are a surefire, quick method for increasing profit.

The downside is that investors usually only look at the upsides of micro-cap stocks, while disregarding the negative aspects. Stocks that are worth such a low price can go down just as easily. A lot of the times, these stocks are not successful, meaning that there is a high chance you could lose your investments.

To summarize, certain companies on pink sheets and on the OTCBB are great quality, and some of the companies on the OTCBB work very hard to get to their positions on NYSE or NASDAQ. But, there are lots of great chances for stock out there that trade for higher amounts.

This doesn't mean that penny stocks are a lost cause, just that they involve a lot of risk that aren't appropriate for all investors. It's important to know whether penny stocks are right for you before deciding to jump into them, and the best way to do that is to do plenty of research before making any decisions.

Another way to decide whether or not penny stocks are right for you is to do practice trades with fake money, which we will cover in more detail in a later chapter of this book.

Chapter 2: Penny Stock Concepts

After reading the first chapter, you may be very excited to jump into trading penny stocks, but you'll have to slow down a bit, first, to learn some important concepts about it. This chapter is about what you need to know before deciding to trade for yourself. Part of getting to know about these stocks is researching plenty of information about them, meaning you will come across words you have never heard before. Hopefully this chapter will help you be more prepared for that situation:

- Buy: This is a simple one to start out with. If you have any familiarity whatsoever with how stocks work, you likely are already aware that buying means you are taking a position, or buying a company's shares.

- Sell: In a similar vein, selling refers to getting rid of the shares you bought with the order, because you have either accomplished your goal of trading (exactly what you want), or because your stock isn't doing as well as you hoped and you need to minimize your losses (the less desirable situation).

- Short selling: Many traders of stock put their focus on going long, which we will define next, but it's also possible to make money with short selling. This means that you contact your broker to borrow shares, assuming or hoping that the stock will go down in price, and then buy to make up for the position. Since a lot of penny stocks are destined to fall, it's possible to make income on this alone.

- Going long with penny stocks: You can earn income when stocks are gaining and also when it is falling in value. When you "go long", it means that you make money from a stock gaining value. Essentially, you are counting on the stock of the company going up so you can buy it at a low price and sell it for more.

☐ Cover buying: When you take a negative position and sell short, you will have to buy back to pay your trader back and to cover your purchases. Share price differences between first selling short and buying to cover is what you end up making in profit from trading.

☐ Market order: A market order essentially is making the statement that you like a stock so much that you are willing to purchase it, no matter how much it costs. This might be effective if you are trading chips, but with micro-cap stocks, you are attempting to make a profit from cheap share.

Establishing buys as market orders means you are a lot more likely to get screwed over by the market's whims.

☐ Limit order: When you place a limit order for buying, you are setting the precise price that you are willing to put forth for that stock. For example, a limit order might mean that you won't pay more than, say $8 per share for a particular stock. For this reason, it's recommended, especially for beginners, to use limit orders instead of market orders. This doesn't mean that your order will always be filled, but doing this lets you count up what your risk will be.

☐ GTC order (good 'till cancelled): Day orders and GTC orders refer to the length of time your order is still standing. GTC means that it remains until you decide to cancel and it will get executed as soon as the stock is at the price you specify. This applies even to a few weeks ahead.

However, day orders are only good for one day; the day you place them. While you might succeed with either method, day orders can be better since they stay fresh in your mind.

Waiting a few weeks makes it more likely that you will forget about orders. However, if you are very organized, a GTC might work for you since you could choose the perfect time to enter a company without needing to monitor it constantly.

☐ An after-hours or premarket order: The hours for the stock market are 9:30 in the morning to 4 pm Eastern time. However, there is something called premarket that opens at 7 in the morning and runs until 8 at night. You can keep a watch on these periods of time to see if certain stocks will spike, however, jumping into trading these may not be preferable. Since most people who trade do so in the regular hours, there might be a reason they are waiting till the odd hours to do their business.

☐ Bid: A bid is the price you are willing to put forth for any given stock. Consider this like purchasing a house. If you have a certain amount that you are willing to spend on a new house, which is considered the maximum bid, that doesn't change according to the prices of the houses on the market at that time.

☐ Ask: Asking refers to the price that stocks are selling at, at that given moment. Sometimes this will fit nicely with your bid requirements, at other times it won't.

☐ The bid and ask spread: The spread between a bid and ask is the difference between the amount you wish to spend and the amount you wish to make off of the trade. Whatever the amount is has to be reconciled before any transaction can occur, meaning that the seller has to lower their price or the buyer has to raise it.

☐ The bear market: The bear market is the market that investors think the prices will fall in. Many mistakenly believe that it's impossible to earn money with conditions like this, but short sellers know different and profit from these conditions.

☐ The bull market: This is the condition of the market that means that prices of stocks are expected to go up.

☐ Penny stocks: We are going to review this definition again, since it can change depending on who you are speaking with. However, in general, penny stocks trade for less than $5 or even $1 per share. In essence, the prices are this way since the companies are speculative. It can be helpful to think of them as betting on the underdog horse in a race. The odds of the underdog winning compared to the favorite choices of speculators is quite low, but every once in a while, it can happen.

☐ Market volatility: This definition simply refers to how quickly stocks move. The main issue you can see with investors making trades with stocks that are not volatile is the fact that there is not a lot of money to make if stocks don't move a lot. The exception to this is big position trading or leverage related positions.

☐ Liquidity: This is a term you will hear time and time again when trading or reading about stocks, and it refers to how easy it will be getting into or out of stocks, making it a highly important factor of the business.

☐ Pump and dump: Another useful term to know, and something to watch out for, pump and dump refers to a scheme with penny stocks where people promote and talk up the value of a stock to make its price go up artificially. This can be done with phone calls, mailers, press releases, tips on a website, spam e-mail, or more. People who do this promoting can make money off of this by selling and buying at a specific place in this cycle. This means that you can also profit from this if you are aware of which patterns to pay attention to.

☐ Market capitalization: This is the amount that a market believes a company should have its value at. These include a large cap (companies worth over $5 billion), mid-cap (between $1 and $5 billion), the small cap (estimated to be worth up to $1 billion), a micro-cap, which we have mentioned a few times in this book (valued up to $500 million), or a nano-cap, companies that are estimated to be worth less than $100 million.

☐ Public float: You may hear this term used while reading about the SEC filings of a particular company. This refers to the amount of shares that can be traded as soon as shares controlled by insiders are taken away.

☐ Authorized shares: Authorized shares refer to the complete amount of shares that can be traded by a company. This number is always larger than the public float number and the outstanding shares amount (meaning the amount of shares that are already out there).

☐ IPO: This was discussed earlier, but we will review it again to make sure it sticks. An IPO refers to the initial offering for a price, which will occur when private companies switch to public trading to raise funds. These are not the best to get involved in, although they are popular with the press, since they don't supply you with an edge over insiders or other accredited investors that could have accessed the stock before you did.

☐ A secondary offering: When the stock of a company is doing well, they might have another offering with the hopes of selling off more stock and raising more funds. This can be great for a company, but not so great for investors, since they are typically diluting its value for shareholders that are already involved with it.

☐ Mutual funds or hedge funds: These are two types of accounts for investment that you can buy into. These accounts will then turn around to invest those funds into a bunch of other stocks. These are usually talked about as a safe option for investing, but that is debatable. These funds can be putting your funds at risk since they are run by people always hoping to go higher, with no regard to our account value or risks to it. In addition to that, getting into hedge funds requires that you meet very particular standards, so penny stocks are a better choice, easier and safer than mutual funds or hedge funds.

☐ ETFs (or exchange traded funds): These are similar to stocks since they involve buying and selling shares, but are also similar to mutual funds since they use index tracking. These are fine to be involved with, but similar to mutual funds, they won't pay off a lot unless you start with a huge amount of money.

☐ ADRs (or American Depository Receipts): These are for companies from overseas that do their trading in the United States. These do not shift fast, meaning they don't have the liquidity or volatility you should be looking for. In addition to that, you will be betting on markets that offer you no edge. While circumstances do play a role in what areas are better for you, personally, to invest in, skipping these is probably the wiser choice.

☐ Merger: This refers to two companies joining together. Many people wish to get into trades based on news of potential merging, but they don't stop to consider that as one company goes up in value, the other will go down. The problem is that you never know which one will do which, but the advanced technology used by Ivy League traders and computers will know, and competing with that level is not smart or advisable.

☐ A reverse merger: This occurs when a company that is private wishes to have their listing on the stock exchange, without all of the hassle and inconvenience that comes along with the IPO. For this reason, they merge with an already publicly listed company. You will likely discover that many penny stocks are only waiting around to merge with existing private companies.

☐ AMEX and NYSE: These can be compared to the pro league stock exchanges. These are the places where huge and well-regarded businesses conduct their trading. This is not the place for penny stocks or beginner traders.

☐ Grey or Pink Sheets: The grey and pink sheets are where the sketchiest companies can be found, even ones that don't have any show revenue or SEC filings. Much of the information you can discover about these is not even true, meaning that staying away from these might be the wisest choice, especially when they are combined with no volatility and no liquidity.

These are just the basics when it comes to penny stock-related phrases and concepts. Of course, there are many more to learn, which you will come across as you are researching this field and getting to know it better. The more you know, the better you will do with trading penny stocks, and this is a great place to start. You will also be better at following along when you attempt to read articles or books on the subject when you are aware of more terms and their definitions.

Jordon Sykes

Chapter 3: Analysis Techniques

When you're learning about investing in penny stocks, you will have to learn about some analysis techniques, the most famous of which are technical analysis and fundamental analysis. A lot of debate exists for which approach is better, but the short answer is that neither is better than the other. Each has its positives and negatives, and certain lifestyles fit better with one approach or the other. So how do you know which is best for you? Let's cover some beginner information to give you an idea:

Technical Analysis and Fundamental Analysis, the Basics:

A lot of investors perform based on the latter, since they wish to invest in a company that is healthy and has good news releases, quality teams of management, and a market share that is rising. Reading a quality fundamental review can give you all of this information, and more. Other people wish to predict the direction a share price will head by just looking at a chart for trading and using technical analysis, meaning that these investors have less of a reason to be concerned about a company's fundamental characteristics.

Technical analysis, when conducted in a quality fashion, has a lot of advantages over fundamental analysis. But, this technique for trading also has a lot of negative sides to it, and looking at the advantages and disadvantages is always smart before proceeding with any venture. Although it's possible to utilize technical analysis by itself, if you don't add in abstract reviews or fundamental information, you will be worse off. It would be smart to apply technical analysis to whatever research you are conducting in combination with abstract review and full fundamental information, in order to reach the best position of clarity with your research.

Which Situations are Technical Analysis best Reserved for?

☐ When you have less time: Technical analysis can be best utilized when you are looking to get rid of the extra work that comes along with fundamental techniques. Using technical analysis, you don't have to worry about the debt load, revenue growth, market share, or profit margins of a company.

This means you are not choosing to invest in the company, but are instead attempting to gain from your actions involved in the price of the share, using information about what it has done in recent history, up to that point in time.

☐ When you are more interested in short term trading: Another time that using technical analysis is useful is when you are more interested in short term trades rather than long term investing. The majority of investing is involved with fundamental, rather than technical, techniques for analysis.

This means that you will buy into big companies, hoping to make money off of improving operations that make prices go up accordingly. However, if the game of patience isn't really your style, and you hope to see share prices changing fast, technical analysis is more suited for your needs.

☐ You are seeking clarity on buying and selling: When you keep an eye on trade volume, patterns of charts, and the directions of prices, technical analysis can reveal accurate points for selling and buying. Huge volume drop offs, shares that are coming close to resistance levels, or trends that move upward, can all indicate the best times to trade in your penny stocks.

☐ When you need to minimize exposure of your investments: When you have money in stocks, the events that play out in the market have a chance to affect them. When you use technical analysis to trade short term, you have less money sitting there exposed to risk, for the most part. Remember, however, that although shorter frames of time reduce exposure, they do not reduce the risk involved.

If the qualities listed here stand out to you in a positive way, technical analysis will be great for you. This doesn't mean that you need to throw yourself into technical analysis for every decision you make about investing, but it can be a useful tool to add into your trading techniques for penny stocks. A lot of investors who use technical analysis to make their trading choices do not wish to own shares over the course of one night or weekend.

Since events happen when markets close down, and these events can have an effect on the prices of shares when they open back up, day traders and technical analysis investors are subject to the risk of losses. This means that they are usually more cautious about events that could have an effect on the prices of shares, since they cannot react to unexpected changes right away.

The Most Thorough and Effective Method Uses Both Types of Analysis:

The best approach to research deals with a combination of both technical and fundamental reviews. Using fundamental techniques can help you find high quality penny stocks that have operations that are moving in a positive direction. Using technical analysis to read the stocks' trading charts will allow you to find amazing opportunities for buying and making profit. Technical analysis has many benefits, but this method can also have a lot of negative aspects. Being aware of the downsides will help you figure out how to use technical analysis in a smart way, if it does turn out to be right for you.

Some Possible Disadvantages to Consider about Technical Analysis Technique:

☐ Technical analysis has little to do with the actual company: Instead of buying shares in a real company, it's more likely that you are purchasing shares in a possible direction of price. When you are not an investor, but a trader, you might not pay attention to the growth of a company, the increasing of their profits, or whether their competitors are losing business or shutting down. This could mean that you end up selling at inopportune times.

☐ Technical analysis takes a lot of work: People who mainly rely on technical analysis need to look at countless charts every single week. Even doing this, it's possible that they may not find any great opportunities for trading, since a lot of this analysis doesn't reveal predictable trends much of the time. Traders who dedicate a lot of their time to looking at charts, on average, do a lot better than traders who don't bother putting in that extra time and effort.

☐ It takes quite a bit of time: In addition to a lot of work reading charts, the technical analysis route requires a huge time investment, sometimes as much as a full time job. A lot of that time must be dedicated to corresponding with the open hours of the stock market, meaning you are tied to specific working hours of the day.

☐ It's difficult to predict: Every investor utilizes a different technical analysis tool and uses them in a different way. This means that they also have unique ideas about which indicators on a chart work the best and also which levels of gains are best to take. Adopting this way of thinking, you will have to choose your own indications and tailor your methods for technical analysis as you go along. Even doing this, you can't know for sure that it will work out in your favor.

☐ You could miss out on huge gains: Since most of this type of analysis deals with small gains in higher frequency, you could end up missing out on big moves, like the 100 or even 1,000 percent moves. Just one penny stock that goes up drastically in price could offer you more profit than taking gains and losses at 20 percent for years in a row.

Regardless of the type of analysis you favor, or whether you end up using both most of the time, there are a few qualities to keep in mind for improving your trading techniques.

Keep these in Mind at all Times with your Analysis:

☐ Instincts: You can train your instincts, but it is never a quick process. You can shorten this time by reading about the subject a lot, talking with people who have more experience than you, and committing to constant improvement. Skills, knowledge, and practice are the best way to develop your trading instincts. Even taking this into consideration, not everyone is equal, because they have differing ways of thinking. While some are naturally talented, others have to work harder.

☐ Practice: It isn't as simple as reading about this material for a week or two and then expecting yourself to be a pro. Interacting on a regular basis will help your skills stay sharp. To expect it to be as easy as hanging around the pros for a little while and then becoming one of them just like that is to devalue all of the hard work that goes into mastering a skill.

☐ Consider the effect of bias: Using data points and high numbers can aid you in arriving at a reliable average, but this only works for objective matters, and this doesn't always apply to the stock market. The stock market can be quite insular and subject to huge feedback loops. For an example, think about a piece of news that appears promising for a particular stock. You could read information about that and then favor that stock, suddenly.

This can lead to you talking about it on forums or in chat rooms, seeking out advice on the matter, and reading the opinions of others who agree with you or are also excited about the stock. Since everyone received the same information and are giving it back to each other, it seems credible, but these qualities don't make for strong evidence.

To summarize, the best way to become adept at a skill is to dedicate yourself to practicing it, mastering it, and staying realistic. Don't fall prey to the temptation of get rich quick schemes or assume that penny stocks are a fast way to win big and quit your job next week. These are the assumptions that lead people into starting a venture and quitting fast because it didn't live up to their huge expectations. Like any other skill, trading stocks takes time to build if it is going to be of any value.

Take your time; learn about exactly what fundamental analysis means, what technical analysis means, and which is better for you. Even if you decide to specialize in and focus on one over the other, the best and most successful traders utilize both to get a more balanced picture and increase their chances of winning and profiting. Remember that however far you advance, there is always room to move up.

Chapter 4: How to be a Penny Stock Pro

For every corporation that is traded publicly with capitalization of the market in huge amounts of money, there are countless other small companies with market caps that are a lot more modest.

Since these companies don't have as big of operations or risks as others, they can be traded at much lower prices. I am talking, of course, about penny stocks. In this chapter, we will go over some of the dangers to stay aware of if you desire to become a penny stock pro.

Factors to Stay Aware of when Mastering Penny Stocks:

☐ Beware of the myth of the evolving stock: Something that keeps people coming back time and time again to dabble with penny stocks is the assumption that the companies will grow and evolve into something huge and great. Although this is possible and happens sometimes, it isn't as common as proponents of penny stocks want you to think.

A lot of public firms choose not to go public until they have reached a big enough stance to make it worth it. Until this happens, they might opt for raising funds using corporate loans or private investors in addition to their typical operation methods. In general, these companies won't need IPOs (or initial public offerings) to fund their growth. The bigger a company gets, the more it makes sense to raise money using public offerings. This is because, even though equity can be seen as the expensive option for financing, it is the better and more necessary option for big corporations.

☐ Pure intentions in penny stocks? When companies offer their stock out at penny stock prices, it's typically due to one of these reasons. It could be because they are on the verge of a huge expenditure and thinks that funds raised from an IPO could be the amount needed to finance this expenditure. Or, it could be because they have reached an apex in their size and want to disperse their earnings or shift the structure of their taxes.

In addition to those two reasons, there are some reasons that a company could opt for IPO when they aren't big yet that are less noble. It could be because a company has been convinced into being involved with an IPO that is overhyped and overpriced by brokerage firms hoping to make a quick buck by taking advantage of investors. It could also be the company owner's attempt to shift their ownership of the company over to others because they don't see a bright future for the business.

☐ Comparing apples and oranges: It's a good idea to keep in mind that there are a huge range of companies within penny stocks and that the variance is immense. You could, for example, see a corporate structured company that specializes in prospecting oil right next to a farm that is family run and specialize in crops.

Some businesses like these let investors chime in and give their opinion on who runs the show, while others are operations run by one person that fall apart when that person decides to retire. Bigger companies, on average, wish to please people who invest in them, and companies using penny stocks don't always care about this aspect of the field.

How to Increase your Effectiveness and Skill in Penny Stocks:

A lot of great companies start out trading with penny stocks, meaning that choosing to invest in these companies can pay off huge as they grow into larger stocks. But penny stocks don't typically have a positive name in the investment field, and, at times, this is for very good reasons. However, once you figure out a few methods for avoiding the negative possibilities of getting involved in penny stocks, you can find great companies that can pay off into fantastic rewards in the future.

Protection from the Downfalls of Investing in Penny Stocks:

People who decide to invest, but don't learn about the most effective methods of protecting themselves from the risks that come along with penny stocks might end up getting burned. However, if you follow the points below, you will be able to avoid most scams, bad investments, and faulty information:

- ☐ Stick to higher caliber markets when possible: For the safest bets, try to stick with AMEX, NASDAQ, and OTCBB for your penny stock trading. While low caliber markets like OTC and

   Pink Sheets can hold promise, it isn't worth the risk when you are first starting out.

- ☐ Do research and reach your own conclusions: Although well-meaning friends or family members might have a tip for you, you should never operate based on that alone. Remember to always do research on your own and reach an informed conclusion before investing to avoid losses and maximize success with penny stocks.

- ☐ Stay away from free stock picks: Don't ever pursue these, no matter how alluring they may seem. When you hear about a stock through e-mail, a mailing list, or a free newsletter, they typically have some type of hidden motive. They will try to trick people into buying stock using tactics and false information, planning to get rid of the shares after convincing enough investors to trust them.

☐ Stick to solid stocks: You should only get involved with penny stocks that have solid fundamentals. If you aren't sure how to find this out, you can quickly find the information you need by looking up the company online. Do a check for the position of their financial situation and make a choice based on that.

☐ Be wary of story stocks: Watch out for stocks that come along with an incredible story. Very bad investments can have great business concepts, like the curing of a horrid disease, or an engine design that will solve the pollution issues of our planet. But stocks with fantastic stories such as these are most often bad companies in terms of finances, and the tempting nature of their concepts of business will have pushed their value way higher than it is really worth.

☐ Don't be afraid to call and ask: The more you know the better. This means that calling investor relations phone numbers for the company you're looking into is a great idea. They should be more than happy to answer your questions, and knowing which ones to ask can allow you to discover quite easily how legitimate the business really is.

Using all of these tips will help you head in the right direction for becoming great at penny stocks. Now that we have gone over some of the qualities to look out for to become a pro at penny stocks, we can look for what to gravitate toward to enjoy success.

Criteria to Look for in Quality Penny Stocks:

When you come upon penny stocks that have these traits, you have likely found a valuable investment that will grow and continue to grow in the future:

- A reputable team for management: Quality penny stocks will have a quality management team. The best way to determine this is to look into how successful they were with prior businesses, which will be a good indicator for future success, as well.

- Quality property intellectually: This means copyrights, trademarks, and patents that will survive against competitors. Quality in this regard can be easy to spot, and if not, some research will tell you all you need to know about what to look for.

- Quality marketing techniques: A wise investment choice will have effective marketing tactics that accentuate their brand and also prove to earn profits.

If you do your research on a company offering penny stocks and find that all of the above is in order, you have found a great opportunity. A lot of this information can be found online with a quick search about the company.

A Method for getting Great at Investing in Penny Stocks:

It's possible to practice your trading tactics in legitimate stocks, in legitimate time, without risking any money. This is referred to as "paper trading" and involves using fake money for real stocks and learning by staying on top of how your picks do.

When you use this method, you can improve at investing in penny stocks quite fast. The best part about this method is that improving doesn't mean you have to risk actual money. As soon as you have reached a comfortable position in your investment knowledge and enjoy consistent profit with your fake trades, you can confidently switch to using real money. Here is how to do it:

- ☐ Begin with a false amount of money: Keep an eye on the current, real penny stocks out there and pick which one you would purchase with real capital.

- ☐ Take notes: Start writing down the trades you would have made, including when you would buy and sell. Make sure to record the name of the stock, the date, the purchase's dollar amount, and prices per share. Be as detailed as you possibly can, you will need these notes later.

- ☐ Invest in multiple: Do this with a lot of different penny stocks instead of only a couple, so you can get the most experience possible using this method. There is no reason to limit yourself to only one or two different practice stocks. The more you have the better and faster you will learn.

- ☐ Record which false investments were profitable: Keep track of your success using fake money so you can figure out what methods of yours are successful and which you might be doing wrong. Write down your successful methods so you know what to do more of and what to ease up on in the future.

If you make it a point to learn as much as possible about penny stocks through daily research, in combination with trading with fake money using real stocks, you should be well on your way to learning the ropes of penny stocks. It won't be long before you are ready to make the jump to real money and start earning profit.

Chapter 5: Risks and Rewards

You could say that penny stock investments come with large risks and large reward potentials. It is possible to earn profit using penny stocks, and there are a couple of main ways to accomplish this, but penny stocks are inherently risky. We have already covered quite a lot of material about the risks they represent. But what is the potential behind investing in penny stocks? What is there to gain from choosing this path?

What are the Reward Potentials of Getting Involved in Penny Stocks?

We should first state here that the tactics we are about to describe have the propensity to work well for some time, but they are likely not sustainable on their own. If you have the desire to earn profit using the stock market, you should invest in companies that are required to file using the SEC, report their net income levels and revenue amounts, and also have healthy balance sheets to show. Penny stocks can be an avenue you pursue on the side of this venture, rather than your main focus.

Consider Investing in Penny Stocks as a Supplement, rather than the Main Focus:

If you wish to be more speculative than this, you can take a look at the stocks that trade above $3 but under $5 and use a major exchange to trade on. There is a lot more winning potential there than with the average penny stock, but you will need to do some serious research to find promising candidates. Some of you, however, may still have your heart set on pursuing penny stocks on their own. If you do decide to pursue penny stocks in addition to or instead of this, your best shot at making a profit is to trade with the existing scheme.

The Quick Method for Making Money with Penny Stocks:

To say it another way, certain investors purchase shares of stock right after getting spam e-mail or junk newsletters, aware that other people will have received it, too. Right away, this will make the trade volume grow and create a more liquid state for the stock, leading to sales for the investor who just made some quick gains. This sounds great on the surface, doesn't it? But there is a risk with this method. On the off chance that your timing is wrong, you could end up losing money.

The Longer Method for Finding Promising Penny Stocks:

There is another option for making money with penny stocks, and this one takes a bit longer. This method involves creating a list of penny stocks and only reading more about the ones that are creating revenue, offer liquid stock, have a real website with legitimate contact info, are cutting losses or making profit, and that either have a quality balance sheet or don't have any debt. This will take almost all penny stocks off the table for you. But, every so often, due to odds, you will come upon something with great potential.

The issue here is that even when you discover a company with great potential that offers you a lot of profit, strong fundamental aspects of the company are not always sustainable long term in these situations, particularly when they are nano or micro-cap companies. This means that this strategy doesn't produce much profit in the long term, and that this method is better suited for short term investing.

In Conclusion:

Some would compare investing in penny stocks to going to a casino and hoping to win. This is because the penny stock environment is full of people who try to scam and scheme, and they have gotten pretty skilled at it. This can translate to less profit for you and more profit for them. In spite of the potential for short term profits and gains, winning long term with penny stocks can be a gamble. If you do decide to continue on with this because it fits your lifestyle and investment personality better, sticking to a profitable method that has been sustainable is the best way to win with penny stocks.

Jordon Sykes

Chapter 6: Penny Stocks or Options Trading?

Are you curious about getting into stock market trading? Typically, someone looking to get started in this does not have unlimited capital to practice with. Due to this fact, they realize that their account won't support trading in huge stocks like Netflix or Microsoft. Because of this, a lot of traders start out on their journey to look for something better that costs less money.

This leads them to penny stocks, which, if done right, can pay off greatly. But how do you know if this is the right choice for you? Have you reviewed options trading? Are you fully aware of the differences between penny and options trading? If you have read this entire book and still don't know for sure, this last chapter should help you make an informed decision. After this section, you should have a better idea of which is right for your personal situation and goals as an investor.

What are the Difference between Penny Stocks and Options Trading?

☐ Commission, fee, and regulation differences: With trading either options or penny stocks, your fees are about the same, if you have a broker. While some brokers can be more suited for penny stocks and others are better with options, if you discover the best broker for your specific wishes, the fees end up being virtually the same.

The difference is that with penny stocks, you may be limited by the ruler of the pattern day trader. This rule only allows you to make three day trades per week when you are using an account with less than $25,000 in it. In options trading, you don't have to use this rule.

So for regulation considerations, options trading is better.

☐ The amount of opportunities for trading: What is specifically meant by the word "opportunities" in this context? In this scenario, it refers to the amount of chances you have to make actual money off of a quality situation for trading. In the world of penny stocks, any specific stock can sit for months with little to no motion whatsoever. It can be difficult to discover this type of stock that moves a fair amount and is appropriate to trade.

Why is that? Because the market of penny stocks is, by nature, not very liquid. This means that activity level of traders is typically low. Traders have to sell and buy to each other to keep the volume going, and this is a problem since there are not a consistent or large number of these stocks. However, options trading is based on ETFs and stocks on the big board, making a consistently high volume daily. This means it's simpler to find chances to make profit off the market.

☐ Potential gains in the world of trading: What draws people into options trading and penny stocks both is the cheap entry and high possibility of gaining. Although there are plenty of risks and disadvantages for penny stocks, they can jump quite high if they get moving.

☐ How much it costs to start trading: In this area, there is a relatively low entry barrier for both penny stocks and options trading. This means that to get involved, you don't have to pay a lot.

For both, a grand or less is enough to start practicing and learning. For this reason, beginners will likely have the best time starting here.

☐ How easy can you sell off the stocks? Trading, buying, and selling successfully comes along with two separate parts. Although this appears obvious on the surface, new traders make the mistake of ignoring it. Keep in mind that it's always possible to buy, but selling means that you must have someone who is interested in buying what you have. This is another downside of penny stocks.

Since there aren't a large number of stocks, it can be hard to find someone who wishes to buy your shares when you wish to get rid of them. Options trading means that there is nearly always at least one person interested in buying what you have. This is another reason that people opt for options trading, rather than getting into the penny stock market.

From this list, it appears as though options trading is the better route to go by, but this doesn't mean that you should stay away from penny stocks. In fact, your specific plan and strategy might be perfectly suited for them. If that's the case, you should definitely go the route of penny stocks. Remember that you can always switch to something else later on if your initial choice doesn't work for you, or do both together. You can also use penny stocks as a practice method before moving on to something else later.

Some traders of penny stocks get tired of waiting for paint to dry as they hope for positions to move faster, so penny stocks aren't right for someone who struggles with patience. Similar to any type of investment, there are pros and cons to buying shares or investing in a company with your own money. You need to be fully aware of what you are involving your money in, whether that is a business nearby or a corporate international giant. While the list above certainly makes options trading out to be the better choice, there are some compelling reasons to opt for penny stocks instead.

☐ Low prices: This one seems very obvious, given the name of penny stocks. In fact, this is what draws in most people who are interested in penny stocks. Their cost per share is very low which means that you don't have to have a lot of money to start investing.

☐ They are common shares: Another great benefit about penny stocks is that it's simple to purchase them since they are common shares, meaning available easily to the main public for purchase. Since these stocks are priced so incredibly low, many different investors can purchase stocks, enhancing options for investors. This means you can invest in a lot of different penny stocks at the same time without needing to worry about how much it will cost you.

☐ Higher profit potential: Another benefit to this type of investment is the potential for making higher amounts of money with investing in penny stocks, for people who know how to monitor the fluctuation of stocks and research the market wisely. This is a skill that can be learned, practiced, and improved over time.

☐ Even if you are not perfect at it at first, you can improve greatly with dedication, time, and practicing with fake money. You can also sign up for practice programs online that are designed to improve your skills immensely. In this field, there is no limit to how high you can climb or how much you can earn.

☐ Fast movement: A lot of people enjoy trading penny stocks in comparison with other stocks because they shift at faster intervals. This means there is a chance of making profit in a very short amount of time. It could happen overnight or within just a few days. Instead of having to wait around forever, you can opt for choices that let you see immediate results. For this reason, some consider penny stocks better for short term investing than for long term investing, but both are possible.

- Multiplying value: At certain times, penny stocks can increase and get traded as something called a mid-cap stock, meaning it can increase exponentially in value. You need to have a few specific qualities if you have any chance of profiting from playing the penny stock market. These qualities include being highly patient, deciding to invest a small amount of capital at first, and acting as intelligent as possible.

You need to receive as much information as you can about a particular stock before getting involved with it. You also must be careful about the broker you decide to go with who can invest your capital with the least risk. This will lead you to better profits at the end of the investment. Anyone who has some knowledge of investing stocks and purchasing shares is aware that it can be a volatile and risky endeavor to get involved in. As we have said multiple times in this penny stocks guide, this type of venture is not for everyone, but with time, effort, and patience, you can become an expert at it and eventually earn yourself a great income. If you do decide to get further into this field, I wish you the best of luck on your journey.

Conclusion

Thank you again for buying this book!

I hope this book was able to help you to feel more knowledgeable about the world of penny stocks. This book was meant to be an overview of the process, suitable for the layman or interested beginner. My hope was that, after reading this guide, you would feel ready to make a decision about getting further into this field.

If you are interested, the next step is to continue researching the subject. While some believe that stocks only work for some and not for others, or require a certain type of intelligence, this is not true, and anyone with a willingness to learn can get into this field. I hope that you found this book interesting and are ready to take the next step on your journey into penny stocks. Although this book is a great starting point, it's far from all you need. You have only just delved into the vast world that is penny stocks with this book. Now you need to seek out specific information about strategies for penny stocks and learn much more about how they work.

Thank you and good luck!

Penny Stocks Strategies

Powerful Strategies to Dominate Stocks

Introduction

I want to thank you and congratulate you for buying the book, "Penny Stocks Strategies".

Mistaken Assumptions about Trading Stocks:

Many people believe that being successful with trading means you have to be a exceptionally intelligent or talented. They believe that only a genius can get rich off of trading penny stocks. The good news is that's not true. This book contains proven steps and strategies on how to master penny stocks, and you don't need to be highly skilled at math or even of above average intelligence to do it.

Who is this Guide Meant for?

However, this book is not meant for everyone. It's only meant for people who have a willingness to try hard and take their trading seriously. While some believe that trading is a shortcut to riches with hardly any work, that simply isn't true, and you don't get anywhere exceptional without effort. The good news is that it doesn't matter if you're a senior citizen or a student in high school. Whether you are someone who can only read about penny stocks for an hour a day or someone who has the time to study the subject for hours a day, a complete newbie to the subject or someone who already has the basics down, this guide can help you.

What does it Take to Succeed with Penny Stocks?

As long as you have a willingness to try hard and put in the time and effort, you can be successful with the information in this book. So how much should you study penny stocks if you wish to master them? As often as possible. If you are serious about becoming a successful trader of penny stocks, every bit of knowledge and information you can find on the subject will get you further along in your goal of acquiring wealth and therefore freedom.

How to Approach this Book and the Knowledge within it:

If you don't have unlimited time, simply take the lessons, chapter by chapter, whenever you can. But as soon as possible, return to the guide, finish it all the way through, and start practicing what you have learned. If this is a subject you are interested in, there's no reason to wait around to get started. Start your journey by reading this guide.

Some of What you will Find in this Guide about Penny Stocks:

When you are reading this guide, you might see a few different perspectives described. This is because investment strategies are as varied as individuals themselves, and there is no "one size fits all" technique for trading. You must, instead, create your very own plan that fits with your personality, lifestyle, and capital, perfectly. The information in this book is not meant to tell you exactly what to do word for word, but inspire you and give you the tools to create your own plans that work for your life. The key is to try out many different methods until you find the one that works for you.

Thanks again for buying this book, I hope you enjoy it!

Chapter 1: How to Invest in Penny Stocks

The appeal of trading penny stocks is not difficult to understand. They are pretty cheap compared to other stocks and hold the allure of large profits in the future. However, if you aren't careful, penny stocks are also a quick way to lose your valuable and hard- earned capital.

Making it your Business to be a Penny Stock Expert, Before Getting Involved:

Of course, it's perfectly possible to profit and win big when you have an understanding of how the game goes, but when you aren't aware of it, the odds are stacked heavily against you. This is especially true when you consider that scammers and manipulators are often the ones running the show of penny stocks.

For people who are interested in investment but cannot afford shares in companies like Microsoft or Google, the possibility of profiting from these types of trades are too tempting to pass up. It is this reason, and more, that the business of trading penny stocks does so well and continues, despite the risks involved. Even with giving a relatively small amount of capital, you can earn a decent profit from the return, as long as the trade goes in your favor.

Promoters of penny stocks always attach disclaimers to their Facebook pages, e-mails, or Twitter accounts, taking advantage of the words they choose to deceive and embellish facts. Promoters of penny stocks also have a tendency to stay ahead of regulations for security. Even considering these facts that make trading penny stocks risky, certain people can't resist the allure of them. So, if you are well aware of the dangers of the lies of penny stock promoters, penny stock newsletters that lie to you, and other risky factors of the game, and still wish to proceed, there are some things you need to remember.

To become Successful with Penny Stocks, Keep in Mind the Following:

1. Don't Pay Attention to Success Stories about Penny Stocks: Experts on penny stocks, people who know all about trading both short and long, tell you that you should never believe the incredible success stories that are fed to people through social media platforms and spam e-mails, however tempting they are.

No matter what, you have to ignore these stories. Get the idea of winning the lottery out of your mind. Looking at penny stocks like golden tickets to riches is the wrong way to approach this subject. Unfortunately, most people do exactly that, and it's what leads them to lose over and over again.

This is part of the reason why penny stocks have a sketchier reputation than others. Instead of viewing these stocks as your tickets to riches, think of them as shady characters that have to earn your trust. Pay attention to the penny stocks that are profitable with solid growth of earnings.

2. Read disclaimers thoroughly and don't pay attention to tips penny stocks are sold a lot more often than they are bought, and it's usually through tips from newsletters and e-mails. Newsletters talking about penny stocks are hardly going to give free tips out for no apparent reason. In fact, if you take the time to actually read the bottom portion of these letters, including disclaimers, you will see that they are being paid to promote certain stocks.

This is because their investors are in need of exposure for their companies. This is not inherently bad, and there is nothing necessarily wrong with needing or desiring exposure, but nearly every newsletter about penny stocks gives you fake promises about low quality companies. There is a distinct difference between stocks earning high for a year straight because of a breakout in earnings and stocks earning high for a year straight because a few newsletters chose it.

A lot of newsletters don't bother to fill you in on the truth since they are being paid to make the stock seem incredible rather than worthless. Falling into the trap of mistaking one for the other can be assuaged quite simply. When you read the bottom portions of these newsletters or e-mails, including the disclaimers, you will often see that there is, somewhere, a conflict of interest happening.

- ☐ Try to Sell Fast: One huge upside of penny stocks is that you can make up to 30 percent profit in just a couple of days. If this happens to you and you earn that type of return, the best guidance you can take is to sell fast. This is where a lot of traders go wrong by getting greedy, hoping and aiming for a huge return, instead of taking what they have already made. Remember that your penny stock choice could just be getting hyped up by promoters, grab your profit, and get out while you can.

4. Don't Listen to the Management of a Company: In the world of penny stock trading, you should never believe what companies tell you right off the bat. You cannot make the mistake of trusting people easily, since companies are just trying to pump their stocks up to raise funds so their company can stay afloat and advance.

Since no accurate data or reliable model for business exists here, a vast number of penny stocks are actually scams or schemes created with the intention of enriching people on the inside of the operation. There have even been instances of big rings of individuals running separate promotions with different companies and press releases.

5. Try not to Sell Short: There are times when shorting

penny stocks that have been pumped up might seem very appealing, but one method that may bring you success is avoiding this temptation. Penny stocks are, by nature, very volatile. This means that if you end up on the worse side of things, it's possible to lose more than half of what you have.

Another issue is it's hard to discover penny stock shares that can be shorted, particularly the ones that make large moves with newsletter tipping and hyped up information. Let the pros do the shorting with penny stocks.

6. Focus your Attention only on High Volume Penny Stocks: You would be wise, especially when you are first starting out with penny stocks, to stick with the ones that trade a minimum of 100k shares each and every day. Trading stocks that have a low volume can make it hard to get out of the position you are in, which is not a desirable situation.

You need to know about the amount of shares being traded along with the volume of dollars involved. You should also look to trade stocks that are worth over 50 cents per share. Any stocks that trade less than that and are worth less than half a dollar, and don't have enough liquidity to be of any value to you.

7. Make sure to Utilize Mental Stops: Due to the spreads on the bid asks of some penny stocks are very high, even up to 10 percent at times, using stop losses in a hard sense can lead to you losing a lot of capital. It does take more effort and focus, but you need to utilize mental stops when you can. By focusing on the risk vs. reward more than stops, you will be in a better position with your penny stocks. Aim for a safe bet and always know what that is before going in.

8. Purchase only the Best of a Group: Choosing to only purchase penny stocks with earnings breakouts under their belt is a wise decision. This means that you buy them when they already have made great earnings or are getting up to a year straight of high volume that has reached a number of shares that is a quarter of a million.

These are not as hard to find as it sounds, as long as you know how to look for them. The hard part can be discovering stocks that have made yearlong highs not from schemes for pumping and dumping, but they do exist.

- ☐ Do not trade your big positions: Something you should always be careful with is the sizing of your positions, otherwise you will have to learn the difficult way that trading big isn't always best. Give yourself a rule to not trade over 10 percent of the daily volume of any given stock. You can also make sure you are limiting the size of your share to give you an easier exit if you need it. Being able to get out of stocks is just as important as getting into the right ones at the right time.

10. Try not to Get Emotionally Attached to a Stock: All penny stock companies out there would have you believe that their story is about to change the way the world works, for the better. When you decide to enter into the world of penny stocks, it pays to be cynical about it. Also make sure you do plenty of research and be diverse about your investments. This applies even when a member of your family or close friend is trying to sell a stock to you.

A lot of people get caught up in with trading their strong emotions, which can hold them back and limit them. The best way to be successful is find out early how to get this under control so you can excel at the game. Also keep in mind that penny stocks have a sketchy reputation and that this has its valid reasons, so always be aware.

Finding Penny Stocks that will Pay you Dividends:

There are not a huge number of these, but some penny stocks do pay you dividends, and discovering them is worth the search. However, this should be seen as a way to supplement your investment returns, rather than a main income source or something bigger.

Using newsletters or websites for finding them:

Websites and newsletters about penny stocks are one of a few different resources that people use to find dividend-paying penny stocks. A simple place to begin is looking through these websites or sources or even subscribing to a newsletter of a credible source that lists penny stocks that pay dividends.

Using Stock Screeners Online to Find Dividend- paying Penny Stocks:

Another way to find dividend-paying penny stocks is by using stock screeners online, many of which are free and easy to use. These can be found on Google Finance, or places like Fool.com or Zacks.com. Utilizing a screener like this is a great way to discover long lists of penny stocks that may pay dividends. As soon as you, as the investor, make a list of your own, you can do the research necessary to figure out whether the individual stock will suit your personal strategies for investing. This process is quite easy:

Make sure to Screen Everything Out that is not Stocks:

Make sure that your screening process isn't including in it ETFs or mutual funds.

Screen Stocks out that Sell for over $5 per Share:
While individual strategies are the best method for this and investors can decide on the appropriate dollar amount for their personal plan, this is a good guideline to work with when starting out.

You will see that the next available screen has refined your search results to what you need to see; this means stocks that have payout ratios for dividends that are over 0 percent. As soon as this refinement has been applied to the search, you will have at your fingertips a list of stocks that offer dividends. Usually, this type of search will reveal up to 100 different stocks for you to look over and consider. These results can be refined even further by adding filters like volume of trading minimums. This is useful because one common issue with trading penny stocks is trouble with finding liquidity.

Great Advice and Information about Penny Stock Trading:

Although penny stocks are usually defined by having a selling price of under $1 for each share, inflation affects this definition every so often, shaking up what the meaning of a penny stock really is. This means that penny stocks usually refer to stocks that sell under $5 for each share. What this means is that some stocks, even the ones traded on major exchanges like NASDAQ and NYSE can still be called penny stocks. However, most of what traders call penny stocks are traded using Pink Sheets or the OTCBB.

Some Information on Pink Sheets Penny Stocks:

Stocks being traded through the former, which is basically just a service for quotations, do not have to register with the SEC, or the Securities Exchange Commission, which means that they are basically not regulated. This means that they are the riskiest of all of the penny stocks that an investor can get involved with.

Some Information on OTCBB Penny Stocks:

The stocks being traded on the OTCBB are typically a lot easier to find good information about and conduct research on. However, even these penny stocks are not as regulated as major exchange featured stocks, like the stocks on NYSE. A lot of the research and information found on these could be false hype that can't be logically trusted.

Because of the high risks that come along with the world of penny stock trading, discovering the stocks that do pay dividends will do a lot to help investors maximize and preserve their investment funding. A lot of penny stocks don't fail completely; they just don't do much of anything, in general. The price of a penny stock could even stay unchanged, essentially, for up to a year or even longer. When this situation occurs, the yearly dividend of even very low priced shares can help improve the loss and profit position of an investor.

Chapter 2: Tips for Investing

The rules that you should trade using are rules that will turn the game of penny stocks, which is commonly known as risky and unpredictable, into something that can be more consistent and even predictable. These tips can turn the world of penny stock trading into a venture that offers you profit every week, as plenty of penny stock traders have discovered for themselves after using this knowledge.

There is a lot of misinformation online, which everyone knows, so having a willingness to find truly beneficial information is great, and you should be proud. If you can follow along with the tips in this chapter, you will be saving yourself a lot of headache, time, and hassle. You will also avoid losing money, which everyone wants to do.

Penny Stock Trading Tips to Abide by:

☐ Get rid of your idealistic visions of perfection: People who promote penny stocks don't hesitate to tell you huge stories about businesses that are just about to get huge and revolutionize the entire world with their services. The problem here is that they are usually lying. If the companies involved in these penny stocks were real companies, they probably wouldn't be involved in penny stocks in the first place. They would be on AMEX or NYSE getting traded, where the other companies that meet filing standards go. They would be selling at higher prices instead of being priced like lottery tickets.

The truth is that most of the companies that are penny stocks are destined to fail, and the chances that you will be able to spot the tiny percentage that end up growing with time are not in your favor. This means that you need to stop buying into idealistic stories, believing what you hear. You must realize the truth about trading penny stocks in order to have any success with them.

☐ Shift the expectations of your profit numbers: Another factor to look out for is the hype that promoters of penny stocks will give you about how fast your capital can expand and grow. Sure, penny stocks going from a dollar to 10 dollars is possible, and it is also possible that your money will double or triple in one move. But how much should you actually be aiming for? Think more .75 cents.

While you can be happy with making more than this, committing to keeping your trades modestly small, and getting yourself into and out of them when the numbers are in good order, is the better option. This will help protect you from the possibility of disaster and huge losses that plague so many other traders. If you are always in the mindset of going after huge wins, you will find yourself forcing trades that might not even exist. This is the type of mindset that will force you out of the race before you've had a chance to begin.

☐ Always respect the Reality of risk: One of the necessary components of managing to keep your profits (and what you lose) small is having respect for the risk involved in trading penny stocks. Oftentimes, companies that are penny stocks are not worth basic paper. Penny stocks are traded thinly since they are known for being very volatile. It is better to take your profits and losses too fast than too slow.

Stocks that you believe are heading up can go down in less than a couple of minutes, while stocks that you believe will sell short for sure can switch course faster than you can blink. A huge factor in how risky penny stocks can be is because of the fact that a lot of the companies could not meet the requirements for filing SEC; and that the individuals trading them are not big time Wall Street people, meaning they can more easily manipulate the stocks if they desire to do so. This is why penny stocks get traded on OTCBB and Pink Sheets. If they could, they would be on the big exchanges instead.

What it comes down to is that you have no way to know for sure what you are handling when it's about penny stock trading. It's possible that the press releases you see about the new technology of a company could be legitimate, but it's also possible that these are lies invented by a promoter trying to hype up the stock. This risk is just part of the game, and not something to fight. You can, however, respect the risk.

Be sure to never commit too large of a portion of your investing portfolio to one single trade, and also ensure that whichever position you're taking isn't big enough to have an effect on the price action of the stock. Always be on the lookout for quality liquidity in penny stocks, meaning a minimum of 100k shares traded per day to give you a good amount of volume for trading. This is the only way you will be able to go into and out of trades as you need.

- ☐ Using a journal for trading: When you start trading as a beginner, a huge favor you can do for yourself is to make a journal for trading that mentions every move you make, the size of the positions you take, the profits or losses of your trades, and more. This journal will serve as a valuable teacher about both your own habits and attitudes and trading, in general. This is a must if you wish to become a trader who profits consistently.

The traders who enjoy the most consistent success have methodical strategies. They never enter trades or make a play on momentary whims. Instead, they consider their actions of the past careful and use that experience to enhance their future actions. Recorded info about your trades from the past will be extremely useful to you as you seek to move up in trading penny stocks.

If you want to maximize the usefulness of this tool, you should track your actions from the very beginning. Get into the habit now, while you are still new to penny stock trading. You can go the old-fashioned route and use a paper and pencil, or utilize an app to record your information. Whichever way you decide to do it, make a commitment to keep and update your diary each time you take action with a stock.

- ☐ Don't get so wrapped up in the game that you neglect your own health: People can get so obsessed with this world that they end up completely forgetting about other areas of life, like physical health. Some traders even put on a lot of weight or take up bad diet habits in the name of trading day and night. Don't make this mistake!

Sure, making money is great. Sure, learning about and practicing trading penny stocks can be so much fun that you get wrapped up and forget other aspects of life, but none of this matters if you are not healthy. Don't get so wrapped up in the world of stocks that you forget to get outside and eat healthy meals regularly. You will be mentally sharp, and consequently a better trader, if you prioritize your health; but you will also live longer to do more trades this way. Get rid of your bad habits right now as you are beginning your penny stock trading career so that you can rely on your health for the entirety of your career.

☐ Don't be afraid to invest in knowledge: Once you start learning the ropes of trading, you may be tempted to fall into a rut of believing you know all there is to know, or that you've learned most of the tricks of the trade. But, no matter how much you learn, there is always more knowledge to gain, and there is always someone above your level, no matter how good you get.

For these reasons, and others, you should make a trading education a big priority. Seek out individuals who have done exactly what you wish to do in your trading career and start learning from them as soon as possible. This way, you have a better chance of becoming the best-informed and strongest trader version of yourself.

☐ Figure out how to spot quality sources for learning: It's a safe estimate to say that only a tenth of the traders that exist out there are profitable consistently in their pursuits. Don't pay attention to what traders who refuse to be transparent claim in message boards or chat rooms.

The fact is, almost all traders are going to say that they make money consistently, particularly when they are trying to get you to buy something from them. This makes it all the more important to figure out how to select your teachers in a careful fashion. So, how do you find the legitimate teachers among the scammers? The key is looking for transparency.

☐ Don't be afraid to ask for proof of amazing claims: If you have found a trading teacher that can't stop bragging about their giant profits or all the ways they are going to show you how to win millions, don't hesitate to ask to see proof of this. This can be tax statements or records of the trades they have won big on. You should know ahead of time that in most cases, you will either get ignored or receive an excuse about why they cannot show you this information. Do you recall the journal tip I gave you earlier in this chapter? Traders who are truly successful aren't hesitant about sharing this information with other people.

A lot of teachers of trading refuse to show you this info, and if that is the case with a trainer you've found, you should be skeptical, at the very least. In fact, this would cause many people to walk away from the person altogether. Time is more valuable than that, and your hard earned money didn't grow on a tree. Have respect for the journey, your capital, and trading information and take the time to select a real, legitimate, and honest teacher who will be transparent with you.

Chapter 3: Common Mistakes and How to Avoid Them

With the charts, formulas, jargon, and slang of Wall Street that comes along with investing, doing this on the internet can seem like an intimidating and even scary venture. For certain investors, the idea of taking on the management of their own money is enough to overwhelm. The fear of losing capital due to making mistakes is a lot to handle. Luckily, most of these mistakes can be pinned neatly down into one of the following categories, and thus avoided with the appropriate knowledge and practice.

The Most Common Mistakes with Penny Stock Investing:

☐ Selling and buying too often: A big plus side to investing online is the fact that it allows investors to sell and buy stocks when they decide to do so. The downside, however, is that some of them make this constant access part of their permanent portfolio, making trading stocks into more of a liability than anything else. Having access constantly can turn certain investors into obsessives who can't stop trading even when they want to.

☐ Cutting the winners off too soon and letting the losers run on: The nature of the human mind can be, in some cases, your worst source of sabotage when it comes to investing in penny stocks on the internet. People tend to react in certain ways when they face particular circumstances, and a lot of those reactions end up working against you with your investments. A couple of these elements of the human mind are holding out for bad choices for far too long, and trying to cash in on positive choices far too soon.

When an investor buys a certain stock that goes down soon after, it commonly happens that he holds onto it far past the time he should have let it go, in hopes that it will return due to the quality of the company. When you go down the road of purchasing individual stocks, you have to commit to cutting losses early on. Decide on a percentage that you can stand to risk and stand by that percentage. You can then utilize protective puts and stop orders for the market.

The opposite extreme is also possible, when investors make the mistake of chasing in too soon on their stocks that are winning. Perhaps your allocation for assets is telling you to place 20 percent in markets that are emerging, so you decide to purchase a mutual fund related to an emerging market. If these markets go up in the weeks that follow, but your index fund still makes up 20 percent of your investment portfolio, you should not sell this off to secure the gains you're making. You should, instead, stick with the allocation of your assets.

☐ Placing attention on the price per-share of a stock: One may be tempted to draw conclusions about prices of stocks. But one stock costing $3 and another costing $400 actually doesn't say much about either one of the stocks. The cheaper stock might, in fact, cost more than the higher priced stock because it isn't growing as fast, has more risk involved, or just doesn't earn a lot in relation to the price of its stock.

A per-share price of a given stock only has meaning if you are comparing it to something else entirely. Usually, an investor will multiply a price of a stock by the number of outstanding share to figure out the market capitalization or the market value of a company. The market value of a stock will let you know if the stock is large, medium, or small, and will tell you a lot about the valuation of the stock.

Not keeping track of returns and risks: A lot of mistakes that investors make seem so simple that they are almost surprising. Prudence has a tendency to disappear altogether in the game of investing online. A lot of traders, possibly due to the fact that it takes practice and effort, fail to take their time with seeing the amount of risk they are taking to receive the reward they hope for or expect from stocks.

One of the largest dangers of investing while being unaware of risks and returns is not being aware of whether you are harming your portfolio more than you are helping it. You could be using a lot of your own effort and time purchasing stocks individually, assuming that all that effort is worth it, only to find out that you should have been purchasing and holding mutual funds, instead. Rather than spending hour after hour studying stock chart information, you could be better off using that time to visit family, enjoy hobbies, or work on your career.

☐ Trusting the wrong person's advice: It can be more difficult to not get tips on stocks than it is to get tips. All you have to do is watch television, strike up a conversation with someone next to you on the bus, talk with people in the finance section at the library or local bookstore, or talk with investors on the internet. You will find that you always run into people who have beliefs about what stocks you need to purchase now, since they are about to take off very soon.

Unless you happen to be sitting next to Warren Buffett on the bus, you should probably just nod politely and forget any advice on investing you hear about from others. Stick with the plan you decided on. Other people, while well-intentioned, simply can't know your personal details as well as you do. Only you will know what works best for you.

☐ Attempting to earn too much profit, too fast: When you decide to become an investor, you should realize that capital is gained over time along with companies you have chosen to invest in grow their earnings and revenue. Speaking in general, stocks return up to 1 percent, annually. You might pull off boosting that number a little bit if you are smart with allocating your assets.

However, some investors just don't think that's enough. Instead of being satisfied with their gains, they need to go chasing after IPOs, hoard penny stocks, or chase the leaders of the market. These are typically the investors who get pulled into those schemes for getting rich quick, conferences on stocks, and other promotion scams that only benefit the ones doing the promoting.

☐ Letting your emotions get the best of you: The stock that ends up being your very favorite is the stock that you bought at the perfect time and never suffered any losses with. You will find that you can easily become proud of these stocks. Times of second guessing yourself and doubting your choices make up a lot of the worst choices investors make.

These individuals can get so caught up in their love for a certain stock that they will stand by it, even as it continues to plummet past the point of no return. If you allow your fears of losing and your greed for large profits take over your decisions on investments, it is essentially guaranteed that you will sell and buy at the worst times.

☐ Refusing to take responsibility for your own losses: Absolutely no investor in this world enjoys losing capital on stocks, but it happens to the best of us, here and there. The way you react to this inevitability, however, is what decides who you will be as an investor. Some of them decide to seek out others to blame for their choices, such as websites to advice givers or executives of the company they invested in.

That's the wrong approach and will only slow you down; keeping you back from the immense learning potential that comes inherently in every mistake or failure with trading.

☐ Not being knowledgeable about tax Information for investing: A lot of people who decide to get into investing don't know about, or ignore, the advantages of saving taxes on investing. In fact, investors can enjoy very generous breaks on taxes, if they are simply aware of them. Take the time to talk to an expert when you start getting into investing. Also, keep in mind that these regulations shift yearly.

☐ Failing to move on quickly from mistakes: As an investor, you can't allow mistakes from your past to freeze you into inaction. If you purchased a stock and stuck with it for too long instead of letting it go at the right time, the only way to make this worse is to linger over the mistake. Instead, learn from it and don't repeat the misstep. This is the best way to continually improve and attain the goals you hope to achieve with investing.

Due to the advent of brokerages on the internet, any person that has a bank account and an online connection can start trading in a week or less. This is wonderful because it gives people the tools to get into investing on their own instead of needing to rely on experts or mutual funds for investing. But there are a few mistakes that are made by investors who are new to the game that should be kept in mind:

☐ Jumping headfirst into a trade: It's easy to get the hang of investment when just considering the basic theories of buying as low as you can and selling as high as you can. However, in practice, you need to be aware of what these definitions really refer to. Keep in mind that what a seller considers high might be called low to a certain buyer in specific circumstances. This should show you the way differing conclusions can be made from the very same info.

Due to the nature of the relative market of stocks, you need to study as much as you can before diving into it. You should, at least, be aware of the basics like dividend yields, book values, the ratio for price and earnings, and more. Figure out how each of these is determined, and what the weaknesses are and where they are.

And as you are making it a point to learn these terms, you can begin with fake money in a simulator for stocks. It's more than likely that you will discover that the real market is far more complicated than what can be expressed by a couple of ratios, but testing these out on a demo profile will help you advance to new levels in your journey.

Keep in mind that thinking of stocks in terms of percentages instead of dollar values is the best way to go about it.

- ☐ Basing everything on one single investment: Deciding to invest all of your money in one investment is typically not a great idea. Even the greatest companies out there can encounter unforeseen problems and watch the stocks go down drastically as a result of that. Sure, there is a lot more potential for great gains when you put all of your eggs into one basket, but you are also encountering a huge amount of risk. Particularly if you are investing for the first time, you should purchase a multitude of types of stocks. This means that you can learn lessons as you go that are valuable but not devastating.

- ☐ Using cash you cannot lose for investments: Studies have proven that the money you place in the market in large amounts instead of in smaller amounts has a better return overall, but that does not mean that it's wise to invest all you have at the same time.

Investing is something you should get into with considerations for the future, whether you trade or you invest using buying and holding. This means that remaining involved requires capital on the side that can be used for opportunities and unforeseen emergency situations. While having extra money on the side won't earn you any profit or a return, having all of your capital invested is so risky that even the most professional of investors don't do it.

If your situation is only having enough money for investment or just using an emergency money account, you are not in the right place financially to be investing. It simply doesn't make sense in those situations. This is the type of investing that will lead to mistakes based on biases in your behavior and added the added risk of mistake-making is the last thing you want. There is already enough room for mistakes, especially when you are just starting out, without that added element.

- ☐ Relying too much on news about stocks: Whether you are hoping to find out which company will turn out to be the next Microsoft, finding quick hot stock tips to invest in, or following a clue about earth shattering profits; using news as a source for what to invest in is a horrible idea for you if you are new to the world of investing. Keep in mind that you are in competition with professionals that have access to information instantly and know exactly how it needs to be analyzed.

The absolute best you can hope for in that situation is to be lucky and hope that it keeps happening, but that is unlikely to happen continuously. The worst you can fear is getting stuck entering too late, or even following a rumor that has no basis in reality, and over, before you decide to abandon investing in general. Instead of following these news stories or possibly false rumors, your ideal beginner investments involve companies that you have an understanding of. If you also have experience personally in dealing with the company, that's even better.

You would never continuously bet on black when going to a casino with the hopes of earning profits long term, so doing this with investing doesn't make any sense either.

In Summary:

Keep in mind that when you decide to buy stocks personally on the market, this makes you in competition with huge mutual funds.

The people involved in this are investors who make this their full-time business, and it's done with a lot more information and resources than you or the average individual has access to. As you start out with investing, although it may be tempting to do otherwise, you should always begin small and only take risks using capital you won't suffer from losing. Starting too big or using money you can't afford to lose can mean that the market is harsh to you, and you may get so burned that you want to swear off investing altogether.

Once you start getting more familiar with how this field works, the most reliable ways to get quality information, your own tactics and more, you can start investing larger amounts and working with more money. A lot of people get into investing only to lose interest quickly because they do it wrong, investing too much at once, gambling on the market, or using false information in hopes of winning. It's a wise idea to invest by yourself, to find out more about how the market works. However, make sure you are investing in areas you are familiar with and always aim for stocks that have quality that you would like to hold onto for longer time periods.

Sure, it sounds appealing to make money fast, and lots of it, but that's just not how this works.

Like any other field, earning real profits comes over time from slowly building up your earnings. If you are viewing investing with the attitude of lots of money fast for little work, you may want to either reconsider getting into this or step back and think it over or wait until you are ready.

Chapter 4: Short Term Investing

Short term investing refers to holding investments for a few days to a few years before getting rid of them, in hopes for making a profit (of course). This typically takes a more active approach with watching the market closely and often as opposed to allow your money to sit and being able to forget about it for periods of time. Here are some ways you can benefit from investing in stocks short term, and heighten your chances and amounts of returns.

Investing Short Term, the Basics:

Someone who prefers to hold onto securities for just weeks or months at once (at times longer if it turns out the shares perform better than expected) is known as a swing trader. These types of traders get into the market typically only when it is going in their preferred direction, being sure to exist when the activities stop showing these types of trends. For example, a business that has been making top earnings for more than a year could be still held onto by a swing trader, since the stock continues to earn. It simply wouldn't make sense to hold onto it if it wasn't earning, right? As it turns out, it's not quite that simple.

This can be Considered a Somewhat Controversial Investment Style:

There is, actually, a better answer to the question asked above. Investing for the short term is an endeavor that involves high risk, as many advisors in the financial field will warn you. If you look at the rolling average of 15 years on stocks that are small cap, an index fund, or mutual fund, you will see that the chances of an investor making strong profits over the course of a decade is almost 90%. However, if you decide to invest for short term instead, you could be gambling or taking a large risk.

This is because investors who invest short time need to make sure they are timing the market as exactly as they can, essentially trying to predict what is going to happen in a small amount of time. This means that they must buy stocks, as quickly as they can, at their lowest rating and then turn around and sell them when they are at their highest. This doesn't give the stocks a lot of opportunities to come to a balance with their lows and highs. However, investing in the short term does have some distinct advantages to it, as long as you know about which risks come along with it and possess a quality strategy or have a quality, knowledgeable consultant to go to for advice.

Short Term Investments, the Advantages:

If, when you are starting out with penny stocks, you have less of a time horizon to work with, it's possible to benefit from intermediate pricing trends of the market, say, a few months to nine months, and get rid of risks, at least partially. Getting rid of these risks includes lessening the chance of volatility for your portfolio, avoiding huge swings in the market that are happening over longer time periods when the market starts showing downward trends.

What Situations is Short Term Investing most Beneficial in?

If you have quality insight into a company or the particular industry you are working with and also think that there are upsides to short term investing, this may prevent, also, needing to have your capital tied up for longer periods of time when you may have the need to deploy or invest it somewhere else. It's highly possible, with the right information, to effectively manage risk and enjoy big returns quite fast. However, there is a lot of disagreement out there, with consideration to the pros and cons, about investing short term versus investing long term.

Everyone has Different Ideas for What is Best:

Everyone out there has different ideas about what works best and why, and any approach will have people who disagree. For example, some managers of money disagree with the approach of Howard Bandy, a man who has created systems for trading and written about the subject in a few different published works of writing. He explains investing and trading with statistic modelling and mathematics. He likes to use the method of first evaluating and taking care of risk factors, then aiming to maximize profits, but only under a specific level of tolerance for risk.

Why can Long Term Investing seem so much Better?

One of the reasons that experts can look to the success, comparatively, of investing long term, is because of a specific period of time that was uniquely positive, after the Second World War. Before the dawning of the new millennium in the year 2000, the market for equities hadn't suffered a bad decade since the 1930s.

What should you Look for in Stocks for Short Term Investing?

According to some experts, the best and most profitable trading methods trade very frequently (up to 30 trades annually). They also only hold for small periods of time (up to about four days or so) and possess a high winning and losing ratio (up to 70 percent, to be precise). As we've mentioned a few times, trading stocks that are highly liquid is recommended, along with looking for funds that are exchange-traded.

You should focus on price actions of stocks that are in the top quarter, meaning that they outperform at least 75% of other stocks within the same peer group, or companies that are about the same size. When you are looking at approaches in an industry, pay attention to what appears to be moving up drastically. When you see a whole group go up at the same time, this is an important indication of a good investment potential. You can look for options that have been struggling for long periods of time but appear to be recovering from that period of struggle. You can make purchases on weaknesses that are short term or based on pullbacks that make sense in terms of longer upward trend motions.

What Qualifies as Short Term Investments that are not Stocks?

Some people aren't big fans of investing short term, especially when they have preferences for focusing on one stock at a time. The risks of losing in this situation are always higher than when you decide to place your bets in a dispersed fashion. This is why people who are interested in short term investing should opt for ETF. What ETF is, is a grouping of securities that have been designed to replicate closely a particular index. These are able to be traded quite easily, similar to stocks, and don't have a high of transaction fees as index funds in the traditional sense.

When a client wants to invest on a basis that is shorter term, for example, needing a holding time that is at least a few years, it may be better to use tactical investing methods. A tactical investing method is defined as a strategy that is shorter term inside of overall allocation of assets. In this specific case, it would refer to the favoring of assets over longer time. One method for doing this is emphasizing differing segments of the market, like a particular portfolio that has exposure to stocks that are large cap and may have up to 4% dedicated to cyber securities and financial emphasis.

When can Rising Interest Rates be a Positive thing to Look for?

You may also be interested in financial sectors when you see interest rates starting to go up, meaning that considering ETFs could be wise in the allocation of your equity. But, depending on the details of your choices, this could be a dangerous, careless, or aggressive choice, since some ETFs are leveraged in this area, meaning that they use debt, playing up losses in addition to gains.

This means that if the sector of finances happens to plummet, double losses can occur. For these reasons, you can use tactics that are part of bigger strategies. Say, making a commitment to stay with a financial industry that is leveraged for up to half a year, considering only its performance on a short term scale, and then revisit that decision later to decide whether or not to stick with it.

Is Short Term Investing Right for your Needs?

Only you know whether short term investing is best for you, and the best way to determine this is learning as much as you can about it. Although guides like this are helpful and a great step in the right direction, they are far from the only information you need to make such an important decision. When you are just starting out with investing, you should explore all of your options thoroughly before committing to any specific path.

Chapter 5: Long Term Investing

Typical investors usually fit into one of the following categories. They are either interested in investing for gains on a short term level, or interested in investing in gains for longer term goals. It may be obvious that both of these categories have their pros and cons, and if you are trading in the United States, tax implications differ for each and are worth looking into when making your choice. But, tax considerations aside, the strategies employed with investing short term versus investing long term can provide you with highly differing earnings and overall experiences. In the last chapter, we reviewed a bit about short term investing. In this article, we will go over some more implications of investing short term and compare those with long term investment considerations.

Some More Information on Investing Short Term:

We just covered this in the last chapter, but let's review some of what investing short term means. Investing this way usually refers to holding onto a specific investment for a short period of time. Some consider this under a year, while others will consider it less than three years. Some investors will take this more extremely, though. For example, day traders try to hold onto investments for a shorter period of time than 24 hours, starting and entering positions in the mornings and trying to exit or close them before they sign off that day or before the market closes.

This is an entirely different strategy than basic investing on a short term level. Using day trading is difficult to become good at and requires plenty of study time, practice, and more to become profitable for the average person. This chapter will compare investors who use short term methods, in regards to investments that last shorter than a year, and also investors who try to trade after only holding onto shares for weeks, months, or even up to two years at a time. Investors who use long term methods, on the other side of this equation are known to hold investments for five year, ten year, or even up to thirty year periods of time.

Selling High after Buying Low:

The main goal of most investors is to make our capital grow. To put it simply, the goal is to earn money. On the surface this sounds easy, just buy low and sell high. However, it's not that simple. People who invest using shorter trading times typically try to purchase stocks when they see that the market is having a low period or if it stands for a quality value amount. Then they attempt to sell it back after some days or even months when its value has gone back up and it promises some profit. As a concept, this sounds great, and like a solid plan that we should all attempt to do. But, as is customary with the subject of investing, this isn't as simple as it sounds on the surface.

Learning how to Time the Market as Well as Possible:

The most profitable way to maximize profits with strategies involved in short term trading is timing the market as well as you can. What this means is buying stocks at their lowest amounts and then selling them back at their highest, just before they drop back down. If you try to sell sooner than you should, you will be losing out on gain potential. However, if you make the opposite mistake and wait too long to sell, it could have negative consequences as well.

Timing the market as well as possible is something that traders who invest professionally have mastered, using advanced data analysis to project what trends will appear. For example, they might use pricing charts from historical times to look for trends that could apply to their current stock. They could make a value for their stocks, the prices they believe they are worth, and hold it up against the price currently. They could also note the values historically. They use this information to construct their plans for trading and investing. Once their stock reaches what they believe is a low point, it's time to initiate a purchase, putting their selling points at the forefront or top of the chart that records expected trending movements.

So, What is the Issue with This Method?

Problems can occur when certain shares don't end up following the trends predicted or expected, which happens all too often. At times, stocks will reach their lowest low, leading the trader to initiate a purchase, and then be forced to look on as the shares plummet even lower. Then, the investor is left to decide whether they should wait longer or sell, losing out on the hoped- for profits. As mentioned previously, the opposite occurrence can happen too, where an investor makes the purchase, sells it for what he believes is the ceiling for the stock, then watches it rise even more, and loses out on his hoped-for potential gains in profit.

Another Possible Issue with This Method:

Another problem that can occur in trading short time is the amount of trading that must happen to have positions constantly opening and closing. Even considering charges for trading that have been discounted, this can turn out to be costly, leading many investors to have trouble breaking even. Since the entire point of investing and trading is earning a profit, this is a disappointment to be avoided whenever possible, at all costs.

What Benefits are Involved in Investing Long Term?

On the other side, traders who utilize long term techniques enjoy fewer fees for trading, since they hold positions for longer time periods. Traders who use short term methods might see investing long term as boring, or at the very least, less exciting. This is okay, especially for beginner investors. But, even professional or highly experienced investors try to use the longer term strategies.

Advice from the Most Credible Expert of Them All:

Even Warren Buffett has been quoted to say that he prefers to hold stocks "forever" as opposed to for limited periods of time. To put it another way, Buffett sees the value in investing using long term methods. He views fluctuations in the market as chances and has made a lot of money by buying stocks from strong business, while others sold from fear of losing out.

What to Look for in Stocks for Long Term Investing:

Investors who wish to use long term strategies should look for companies with proven records showing growth and stability. Although new companies, at certain times, are great choices for long term profits and growth, you involve far less risk when you select companies that have already proven themselves as quality with their track records. You could also go with stocks that have strong histories of paying dividends consistently. Particularly when you can see that the company increases them every so often. Companies that have shown they are committed to paying dividends usually continue to do as they have always done.

A lot of investors will enjoy benefits from stability that investing long term gives. People who are new to the game should look first to long term methods instead of obsessively charting every shift in the market. This doesn't mean you should always purchase stocks and hold onto them "forever" or even for decades. If you notice significant changes in the company or the entire market, of course you should use your head and make the necessary adjustments. But trades should always be conducted using your overall market principles and strategy, not always changing according to the current movements of the market.

More to Keep in Mind about Investing Long Term:

Remember your real goals here and also what "long term" truly means. Some individuals can create careers for themselves and considerable wealth from conducting trades that only last a couple of minutes. For short term trading, making solid plans based on considerable research is the best way to make and follow through with correct plans for investing. Attempting to use guesswork for predicting where the market will head is the best way to head for disaster. In fact, that's more suitable for gambling in Vegas than trading stocks. If you do consider investing short term, use caution and use only a tiny amount of your main capital. For most of you who are interested in trading, thinking of long term in your approaches is the best way to do things.

Remember that the stock market is full of exceptions to every rule, but some principles are more steady than others and hard to argue with. There are certain trends that you will notice pop up time and time again when you embark upon your penny stock trading pursuits that more experienced traders already know about. Luckily, there are some basic guiding words of wisdom you can use to utilize the long term methods most effectively.

Principles to Keep in Mind for Long Term Trading:

☐ Get rid of losers and allow winners to ride free: Over and over, traders take their earnings by selling off the investments they have appreciated, and then turn around to hold onto declining stocks, hoping that the latter will recover. If investors aren't aware of when to let a lower go, it could have devastating consequences. For example, they might watch the stock plummet until it is worth next to nothing. Obviously, the concept of holding onto valuable investments and getting rid of the bad ones makes perfect sense on the surface, but it turns out it's a lot harder in the moment. This information could help.

☐ Allowing winners to ride: Many investors enjoy huge success due to having a small stock number in their portfolio, but with big returns. If your personal principle is selling as soon as stocks have risen in value by a specific number, you might never be able to let a winner ride all the way through. Absolutely no one that sticks strictly to their numbers has had a chance to reach incredible heights.

Try not to underestimate stocks that are doing great by limiting yourself to a pre-decided rule. Especially when you are new to this and haven't yet developed a full understanding of potential, the rules you set for yourself could be arbitrary or, at worst, holding you back from great profits.

- ☐ Getting rid of losers: You can never count on stocks bouncing back once they have started to decline. It's true that you should never underestimate quality stock choices, but it's also true that you need to be realistic about badly performing investments. It can be very difficult to acknowledge losing stocks since you also have to admit you made a mistake of judgment.

However, you need to be as honest as you can when you notice that your stocks are not performing as you hoped it would. Never hold back from swallowing your pride, being humble, and being smart enough to move on before acquiring even more losses. In both of these scenarios, you must judge businesses using your research. In both scenarios, you must decide if prices align with the potential of the future for the business. Keep in mind, however, that you should never allow your fears to maximize your losses or limit what you can earn in profits.

- ☐ Don't let small things get to you: When you make the choice to be an investor who uses long term strategies, you don't need to panic when short term movements happen to your investments. When you pay attention to your investment activity, remember to keep the big picture in mind at all times. Have confidence in your choices and their quality instead of nervous in regards to short term volatility. And don't focus too heavily on the small difference you may save abandoning a market order and using a limit order.

It's true that traders who are active will utilize moment to moment or day to day changes as ways to profit, but long term investing games happen as the result of altogether different movements in the market (movements that happen over the course of years). This means that you should keep your attention on the development of your philosophy for investing through acquiring knowledge.

- Choose your strategy and stay with it: It's true that different investors have different strategies for choosing which stocks they buy and fulfilling goals for investing. There are countless methods for becoming successful in this field, and there is no specific strategy that wins out against all others. But when you discover your personal style, stay with it. Investors who keep switching between strategies will not be able to benefit from the benefits of each type.

- Keep your eyes on your investment future: The hard part of trading and investment is the tendency to want to make the best decisions about unforeseeable events in the future. You should always remember that, though using past data can be helpful in signaling future events, it is the details of those future events that are the most important.

You should always try to make your choices based on the potential of the future of a stock, rather than strictly limiting yourself to what has happened before.

- Find a perspective that considers the long term: Big profits in the short term can appeal to investors, especially investors who are new to the game. However, thinking more in terms of long periods of time will benefit these people more than having a perspective of getting in, making money fast, and getting out quick. That doesn't mean you can't earn money by doing short term active trading, but trading and investing are different methods for gaining profit on the stock market.

Different risks are involved in trading that investors who do the buy and hold method will not experience. In addition to this, traders who are active need to have special skills to be successful at what they do. Neither one of these styles of investing are inherently superior to the other style, they both have their advantages and disadvantages. However, trading actively can be the worse choice for a person who doesn't have enough time, capital to spend, desire, or education to undertake this skill. Again, there is no objective right answer for what is best. Different styles fit with different lives and personalities.

- Keep an open mind whenever possible: A lot of amazing companies operate under names that are of the household variety, but a lot of great investments are not of the household variety. Countless small companies are capable of turning into huge companies very soon. Actually, in history, smaller caps have enjoyed larger returns than their bigger counterparts.

So, what does this mean and how is it relevant to you? It doesn't mean that you are supposed to go out and devote all of your experience and practice to smaller cap stocks, on principle. Instead, you should keep in mind that a lot of great companies exist beyond the well-known successful types, and that forgetting about smaller companies, you could be missing out on some huge profit potentials.

In Conclusion:

Of course, no rule is set in stone with trading, and every solid rule that you operate under should be reached based on your own experience and knowledge. Regardless of that fact, these tips should be very helpful to people who decide to go the route of long term trading. These principles we have gone over (many of which are common sense) will be of great benefit to you and give you beginner insights to the right attitude to approach your investment career with.

Conclusion

Thank you again for buying this book!

I hope this book was able to help you to get your foot in the door of the world of penny stock trading. My goal was to give you as many varied tips as possible, along with general guidelines, to give you the tools to craft your very own strategy, suited personally to your life and financial situation. There is no one magical method for trading penny stocks, since different techniques will work for different people.

The next step is to test out the information given to you in this guide and find out what works for you. It's possible to earn a living and even retire early on what you make trading stocks, but it doesn't come easy. In order to be successful on this journey, you must accept that it takes time, effort, patience, and a constant willingness to learn.

Thank you and good luck!

Penny Stocks

Powerful Advanced Guide to dominate Penny Stocks

Jordon Sykes

Introduction

I want to thank you and congratulate you for downloading the book, *"Powerful Advanced Guide to dominate Penny Stocks"*.

This book contains powerful steps and strategies on how to become an expert in Penny Stock trading. It holds some of the best-kept insider secrets and strategies for picking out Penny Stock winners, thereby getting you closer to your financial goals.

Various complex strategies and concepts pertaining to Penny Stocks are explained in a simple, easy to follow manner in this book. Supported with ample illustrations, charts, and actual examples, this book is guaranteed to bring in a paradigm shift in your understanding about Penny Stocks.

Within these pages, you will find

- ☐ Precisely what a Penny Stock means and where to trade them

- ☐ The importance of brokers and how their commissions can impact your profits – also how to avoid paying huge broker commissions.

- ☐ Why picking a good stock screener is vital.

- ☐ Various Penny Stock trading strategies

- ☐ Concepts about chart reading – candlestick patterns, chart patterns, volume analysis, and technical indicators

- ☐ Expert criteria for entering and exiting stocks

- Numerous Tips and Tricks to figure out Penny Stock winners

You will also learn...

- How to limit your losses and increase your profit margins

- The criteria for selecting a broker that suit your trading style

- Secrets of successful Penny Stock trading

And lots more...

Remember, people spend THOUSANDS on courses to learn even a tenth of what is being disclosed in this advanced book on Penny Stock strategies.

You get the perfect solution by reading this book –learn how to get the top results with the slightest possible effort!

Thanks again for downloading this book, I hope you enjoy it!

Chapter 1: Brief Introduction to Penny Stocks

"Here's the next big Penny Stock about to breakout – grab it before it is too late!"

"Top secret –hottest trending Penny Stocks"

"Double your money in a day using XYZ Penny Stocks"

Sounds familiar? These are just a few samples of promotions related to Penny Stocks found in magazines and newspapers. Chances are also high that you would notice numerous pop-ups of Penny Stock recommendations when browsing the internet.

The term 'Penny Stock' is exceedingly familiar to all. But not many comprehend the inner workings of it. This advanced guide on Penny Stocks covers all aspects of Penny Stocks: the various advantages and risks associated with Penny Stocks, tips to pick out Penny Stock winners, various useful tools, and resources, as well as advanced strategies for entering and exiting trades. So, let's get started right from the basics.

What is a Penny Stock?
Penny Stocks, also known as ***micro-cap stocks*** are simply the shares of a company that trades at very low prices.

Here are a few quick facts about Penny Stocks:

- ☐ Price of a Penny Stock vary from fractions of a penny, or a penny; to a maximum of $5

- ☐ Traders typically choose $1 as the standard for defining Penny Stocks.

- Penny Stocks have very low market capitalization (hence, called micro-caps)

- Although spread across all industries, the majority of Penny Stocks are concentrated in Resources, Medical/Biotech products, and Technology sector.

Types of Penny Stocks
For the sake of convenience, Penny Stocks can be broadly divided into two categories.

Category 1: Stocks of small companies, or that of companies that were started recently.

Category 2: Stocks of older and reputable companies which used to trade above $5, but are currently trading below $5.

Where are Penny Stocks traded?
The Penny Stocks of the **first category** are normally quoted over the counter like

- OTC Bulletin Board, also known as OTCBB

- OTC Link LLC, also known as Pink OTC Markets Inc.

OTCBB

OTC Bulletin Board is an electronic quoting system that is used for buying as well as selling stocks outside of a formal exchange.

OTCBB is a facility of FINRA and combines the quotes from various brokers and market makers across electronic communication networks into one location.

OTC Link LLC

OTC Link LLC or Pink OTC Markets are also similar to OTCBB. They are operated by OTC Markets Group.

They have three tiers depending on the decreasing amount of regulation: OTCQX, OTCQB, and OTC Pink.

The chart below shows a quick summary.

(Fig) Trading of Penny Stocks of Category #1

☐ **OTCQX:** It is also known as the **Best Marketplace**.

OTCQX is basically for recognized investor-focused U.S. as well as international companies.

In order to be eligible for the OTCQX marketplace, companies should

- ☐ Have high financial standards
- ☐ Exhibit acquiescence with U.S. securities laws
- ☐ Be up-to-date in their disclosure
- ☐ Be supported by a professional third-party advisor.

☐ **OTCQB**: It is also known as the ***Venture Marketplace***.

OTCQB is basically for U.S. as well as international companies which are in a developmental stage and incapable of qualifying for OTCQX.

In order to be eligible for the OTCQB marketplace, companies should

- ☐ Be up to date current in their reporting
- ☐ Go through a verification annually
- ☐ Undergo a management certification process.
- ☐ Not be in bankruptcy.
- ☐ Pass a minimum $0.01 bid price test.

- **OTC Pink:** It is also known as the **Open Marketplace.**

  OTC Pink allows trading through any broker, as well as the trading across a wide variety of equity securities.

  There are no eligibility criteria as such for qualifying for OTC Pink. It allows any type of companies – be they in distress, default or even by design.

The Penny Stocks of the **second category** are traded on exchanges like

- NYSE

- NASDAQ

- AMEX etc.

Although the cheap stocks listed on exchanges like NYSE and NASDAQ aren't technically "Penny Stocks", they bring in a lot of the benefits of Penny Stocks without too much risk, since they are all reputable companies.

Advantages of investing in Penny Stocks
Following are some of the advantages provided by Penny Stocks when compared to regular stocks.

#1 High reward ratio: The stock price of Penny Stocks are very low. This means that you can purchase a large amount of Penny Stocks using a fairly small amount of money, leading to higher profits. This is best understood using an example.

Assume that Person 'A' and Person 'B' each has $500 available to invest.

Person 'A' invests in a good Penny Stock which cost $0.10 per stock. On the other hand, Person 'B' invests in a regular stock that cost $20.0 per stock.

The table below shows the profits earned when each sells their stocks for two different hypothetical sell prices. You can see that the profits grow exponentially in the case of Penny Stocks.

Remember that the initial investment amount was same for both Person 'A' as well as Person 'B'. So, what exactly caused this big difference in profits?

Name	Type of Stock	Buy Price	#stocks	Sell Price	Profit Earned	Sell Price2	Profit Earned2
Person A	Penny Stock	$0.10	5000	$0.50	$2,000.00	$1.00	$4,500.00
Person B	Regular Stock	$20.00	25	$40	$500.00	$60	$1,000.00

(Fig) Understanding Reward Ratios of Penny Stocks

The answer lies in the number of shares purchased using the same $500. Person 'A' managed to buy 5000 shares while Person 'B' could purchase just 25 shares using the $500.

This means that for each price move, the profit earned by Person 'A' is a multiple of 5000 shares, while in the case of Person 'B', the price is multiplied by just 25!

dAs you observed, the growth potential of Good Penny Stocks is of an exponential nature. This means that it is possible to make double, triple, quadruple or even more times your investment amount using Penny Stocks within a few weeks to a year.

Penny Stocks thus provides the prospects of strong earnings for traders or investors who carefully enter and exit at the right time.

#2 Possibility of discovering hidden gems: Amongst the Penny Stocks that are listed on OTCBB and OTC Pink, there would be qualified, hardworking companies with very high growth potential. Identifying such companies would result in gaining a high amount of profits as the business ethics as well as management of such companies would be quite sound.

#3 Good learning opportunity for Novice investors: People new to investing can get the feel of the market by investing in Penny Stocks. Doing so will help them grasp the ins and outs pertaining to trading and investing without risking a huge chunk of money. Trading with Penny Stocks would give the novice investors the necessary confidence to trade in stock markets, rather than just demo accounts.

Risks involved in investing in Penny Stocks
Although the lure of the high rewards makes Penny Stocks irresistible, there are also things that warrant caution. Following are some of the risks associated with Penny Stocks. As the saying goes - Forewarned is forearmed!

#1 No clear standards: There are no well-defined standards available for Penny Stocks when compared to other regular stocks. This makes it riskier when compared to investing in regular stocks.

#2 Poor stability: The companies of Penny Stocks *can be closed* without any previous warning at any point in time, causing the buyers to lose money. This lack of stability is yet another risk associated with Penny Stocks.

#3 Unavailability of company information: It is not mandatory for the companies listed in OTC and Pink sheets to issue financial statements. Many of the companies have *no reportable history* as well. As it is not required for the companies to list their assets, the company could be a shell company or a bankrupt one and you wouldn't be aware of it. Hence, the risks associated with buying the Penny Stocks of the company is higher.

#4 Lack of liquidity: When compared to regular stocks, the number of trades done for Penny Stocks are usually lesser. Hence, it would be difficult to easily buy and sell Penny Stocks, as there are a lesser number of sellers and buyers. This is called as the lack of liquidity.

In addition, due to the *low frequency of trading*, it would be difficult to price the Penny Stocks with accuracy. Hence, Penny Stocks are also considered to be *speculative investments*. All these are risks associated with Penny Stocks.

#5 High probability of fraud: Due to the lack of regulations by SEC, Penny Stocks have a higher probability of occurrence of *scams* and swindling schemes.

Now that the basics have been refreshed, let us move on to the advanced concepts of Penny Stocks.

Chapter 2: Penny Stocks – Advanced Concepts

Importance of selecting a good broker
One of the most important aspects of Penny Stock trading – which is almost as crucial as the selection of stocks – is picking out the right broker. This is because the commission paid to a broker can literally break or make your trade. Unfortunately, not many pay heed to this aspect of trading and end up losing a good chunk of money by paying too much broker commissions.

So, what exactly does a broker do? Here's a quick rundown.

- Brokers basically act as an intermediator between sellers and buyers.

- A broker can be a person or a company who executes the buy or sell orders of the investor for a commission.

- The services of a broker also include advice, deliveries, and negotiations.

Types of Penny Stock Brokers

Brokers of Penny Stocks are divided into two categories - Full-service Brokers and Discount brokers.

#1 Full-service Brokers

Following are the services provided by Full-service brokers:

- Provide advice

- Analyze market trends

- Make predictions

- Tax preparation

- Provide tax tips

- Real estate planning

- Retirement planning

The drawback of full-service brokers is that they are very **expensive**. Full-service brokers have the highest commission rate –up to even $100 per trade. Full-service brokers provide a small discount for orders placed online.

Full-service brokers are **best suited for** people having a **complex financial** situation and are also too busy to stay updated on various issues pertaining to their finances.

#2 Discount brokers

Discount brokers are usually called as **online brokers** as they interact with the customers only over the internet, and not face to face at their office location

Following are the characteristics of discount brokers.

- Discount brokers have a lower broker commission when compared to full-service brokers.

- They do not provide advice or analysis.

- They charge a lower amount for orders that are placed online.

- The services provided are limited to just buying and selling orders at a lower commission

- They do not provide investment services, personalized advice, and tax tips

Discount brokers are ***best suited for*** investors who prefer to do their own research. It is also best for ***active traders*** due to their low commission.

How much does the commission rate of a broker cost? Here are some quick facts about broker commission.

- The commission rate of a broker depends on following factors

  o The price of the shares that are being traded

  o The category of underlying security

  o The frequency of trades made

  o The size of an investor's portfolio

- Brokers charge an extra commission when trading Penny Stocks. More than 70% of brokers will have either hidden charges or higher commission rates for trading Penny Stocks.

- The commission rates of different brokers can differ significantly. But the average cost per trade is on an average $7.25 for online brokers. Below are the commission rates of some of the popular brokers

  o TradeKing - $4.95 per trade

- Sharebuilder - $6.95 per trade

- Scottrade - $7 per trade

- SureTrader - $4.95 per trade up to 1000 shares.

- Charles Schwab - $8.95 per trade

- ChoiceTrade - $7 per trade

- TDAmeritrade - $9.99 per trade

- OptionsXpress - $8.95 per trade

Types of Brokerage accounts

For Penny Stocks, there are mainly two types of brokerage accounts - Cash Account and Margin Account.

#1 Cash Account

- Cash account is also called as Type 1 account.

- This is the *traditional* brokerage account.

- The entire cost of the purchase must be deposited by the time of the settlement date.

#2 Margin Account

- Margin account provides the flexibility to *borrow cash* for purchasing stocks using the securities or cash already available in the account as a collateral.

- If losses are incurred, the broker has the *right to sell* the stocks placed as collaterals to regain the money.

☐ For this reason, margin accounts are not recommended for newbies.

Criteria for selecting a Penny Stock Broker
Following are some of the important factors to be considered when selecting a broker for trading Penny Stocks.

☐ **Broker charges:** Check the charges per transaction for the broker. At times, the broker fees shown are valid only for the first month and could charge a higher rate in the later months.

There might also be minimum trading requirements like say, 30 trades a month for availing the lower fees. Always read the fine print before signing the dotted line.

☐ **Restrictions on trading**: Some brokers do not allow the short selling of Penny Stocks. The brokers who do allow these may have a higher margin requirement or would need additional margins. Check for these factors before picking out the broker.

☐ **Extra charges:** Brokers would have additional fees like annual maintenance fees, as well as charges for making money transfers. There might also be charges in the case of account inactivity, or for withdrawing money to bank accounts.

A yearly IRA fees would be charged for the ones with retirement accounts. There might also be volume limits and Surcharges for large orders. All these should be weighed in carefully before choosing the broker.

☐ **Response time:** The phone lines of some brokers would either be busy, or they would never pick up. Some brokers are hence difficult to get ahold of, especially if you need to make a transaction at a specific price or time. Hence it is best to choose a broker who is easily accessible.

☐ **Tools and Software:** An investor is only as good as his tool. It is best to choose brokers with robust trading platforms, mobile apps available for trading on the go, real time streaming of quotes, and other trading tools.

☐ **Market Researches**: Many brokers provide free market research as part of their service.

☐ **Security:** Before choosing a broker, check for their SSL websites and added security features like double verification and security questions. It is always best to go with a broker who is a member of FINRA and SIPC.

How to reduce broker fees: Pro Tips
Paying Broker Commissions can figuratively eat away most of your profits. In case you have a successful trade, the broker fees are deducted from the profits. On the other hand, in case your trade was unsuccessful, you would still need to shell out money for paying the broker in addition to the losses incurred.

But do not be disheartened, for there are ways to reduce paying a high fee to your broker. Here are some top tips to follow for saving money on broker commission.

#1 Avoid too much trading: Do not trade in an obsessive fashion. Always remember that every trade costs money. So, it is best to avoid trading strategies that require too much trading activities (buying and selling multiple times)

#2 Adjust your trading budget so that it includes money for brokerage: Always plan for the exit price of the trade by factoring in the money necessary to cover the broker commission. For instance, if your trade costs $10 in brokerage, exit the trade for at least a $15 profit

Similarly, set your stop loss too with the broker fees (e.g. $10) in mind. If you intend to set $35 as a maximum loss in a trade, exit the trade when the actual loss reaches $25.

#3 Change your broker: Your trading style typically evolves over time. Sometimes, your existing broker might not be providing the best commission for the trading style you have currently adopted. So it is always a good practice to check and reevaluate your existing broker once in a while.

#4 Select simple trading strategies: Always choose the trading strategies that has the least amount of broker commission for every dollar invested. This means that it is best to avoid strategies like double-wide calendar spread!

#5 Avoid deceitful brokers: Despite the regulations set up by National Association of Securities Dealers (NASD) and SEC, there are brokers who deceive investors using unscrupulous practices. In case you find such brokers, it is best to avoid taking up their service.

Below are some of the ways by which these brokers commit fraud. Understanding them would help in avoiding these pitfalls

- ☐ **Churning:** The misuse of the discretionary authority of brokers over user accounts, in order to increase the broker commission through overtrading is called as churning.

  How to identify it? Check for an excessive number of transactions in your trading account, without causing much change in your portfolio's value.

How to avoid it? Use a wrap account to avoid churning.

- *Withholding useful information*: Some unscrupulous brokers withhold beneficial information from investors for increasing their commissions. For instance, take the case of non-sharing of breakpoints with the investors.

  This is best explained with an example.

  Assume that your total investment amount is $3100. Now, if a mutual fund charges 7% for investing any amount less than $3000, and 4% if the investment amount is above $3000, than the threshold amount of $3000 is called as a breakpoint.

  This means that investing the entire $3100 in one mutual fund would give you a lower charge.

  Now, unethical brokers would distribute your $3100 investment in two similar mutual funds in order to earn commissions from both, while cheating you from the benefits of breakpoints.

  In order to avoid it, the investor must keep up with the latest announcements and updates in order to stay ahead in the game.

- *Doing transactions that are damaging to the investor:* Every investor would have a list of do's and dont's to be followed emphatically. But some brokers do not follow these directions.

  For instance, brokers can choose a high-risk trade when the investor is 100% risk averse.

  At times, the broker might invest all money into one stock when the investor prefers a diversified portfolio.

  If any of this sounds like your existing broker, it's time to reevaluate!

The broker commissions would not be too high if you do your research well. If you are using brokers in order to manage highly complex investments, there is no getting around their ridiculous fees. But in case you intend to do most of the research, and do the buying and selling on your own, your broker fees can be brought down to a huge extent.

Important Candlestick Patterns
The candlestick patterns play a very important role in trading the Penny Stocks. Here is a quick overview about candlesticks.

Every candlestick has four important parts – open price, close price, high price, and low price. The lines available at the ends of a candle are called as shadows.

(Fig) Bullish and Bearish Candlesticks

The figure above represents bearish and bullish candlestick. White colored or empty candlesticks mean that the closing price was higher than the opening price. It is called as a bullish candlestick.

On the other hand, a filled, black, or red candlestick is a bearish candlestick. The closing price would be lesser than the opening price for a bearish candlestick.

108

In addition to Bullish and Bearish candlestick, there is also a neutral candlestick pattern called as Doji.

(Fig) Doji – Neutral Candlestick

Dojis are formed when the opening, as well as closing price of the stock, is same for the day. It can look like an inverted cross, cross, or a positive sign. Dojis usually represent an indecision in market direction.

A single candlestick or a combination of two or more candlesticks can be used to identify the bullish or bearish signals for the stock. Thus, candlestick charts can undeniably provide an edge in picking out winning trades. Next, let us examine some of the important bullish and bearish candlestick patterns

Bullish Candlestick patterns

The candlestick patterns that indicate a bullish bias for the market is called as Bullish candlestick patterns.

These patterns can be used for identifying good entry points for a trade. More details about the trading strategy would be explained in the later chapter on Advanced Buy Strategies for Penny Stocks.

Following are some of the important bullish candlestick patterns:

- ☐ Hammer
- ☐ Bullish Engulfing
- ☐ Piercing Line
- ☐ Morning Star
- ☐ Three White Soldiers
- ☐ Bullish Harami/ Harami Cross
- ☐ Bullish Belt Hold
- ☐ Bullish abandoned baby

#1 Hammer: Hammer is a single candlestick pattern typically formed at the end of a bear run, indicating a trend change to Bullish bias. This candlestick will have a long lower shadow, and have a closing at the high price of the day (or nearer to it).

#2 Bullish Engulfing: Bullish engulfing candlestick pattern consists of two candlesticks. The first candle would be a small black candle and it would be followed by a big white candle that would completely engulf the black candle. This pattern usually appears during a downtrend.

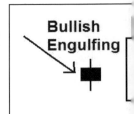

#3 Piercing Line: Piercing Line candlestick pattern is made of two candlesticks and is a bottom formation reversal pattern.

On the first day, a long black candle is formed. On the second day, a white candle is formed whose open price is lower than the close price of first day's candle.

The closing price of the second candle would be within the first day's candle.

Traders pick this pattern and draw a piercing line which cuts through both the candlesticks. Then they enter long positions with a stop loss set to be below the piercing line.

#4 Morning Star: Morning Star candlestick pattern is made of three candlesticks. The first day's candle would be a long black candle.

The second candle would be a small candlestick (white or black). The second candle would start by gaping below the close of the first day's candle. The third candles would be a long white one.

This pattern is helpful in identifying trend changes from bearish to a bullish bias.

#5 Bullish Belt Hold: Bullish Belt Hold candlestick pattern consists of just one candlestick. It is a single white candle

formed during a downtrend which indicates a trend reversal.

The low of the candlestick would be its open price and there would be a price rally during the day, resulting in the closing of the candlestick at the high or very near the high.

A small shadow could be formed at the top of the candle, but not at the bottom.

The strength of reversal depends on the length of the candle's body – longer the body, stronger the reversal!

#6: Bullish Harami, Bullish Harami Cross: Bullish

Harami as well as Bullish Harami Cross are bullish reversal patterns that are made of two candlesticks.

In Bullish Harami Pattern, the first candle would be a

black candle.

The second candle would be a white candle that would have a small body. This second candle would be completely within the range of the first candlestick's body.

In the case of Bullish Harami Cross pattern, there is just one minor difference – the second candlestick would be a doji.

#7 Bullish Abandoned Baby: Bullish Abandoned baby

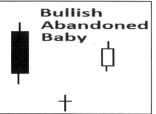

pattern indicates a major bottom reversal and is formed during a downtrend. It consists of three candlesticks.

The first candle would be a black candle.

The second candle would be a Doji. The shadows of the Doji would be seen as gapped below the lower shadow of the first candle.

The third candle would be a white candle. The closing of the third candle would be well into the body of the first candle.

#8 Three White Soldiers: Three White Soldier Pattern indicates a strong reversal signal. This pattern consists of three candles. All the three candles would be a white candle that would be either of a normal size or long. The three candles would move upwards.
 The open price of each candle would be lower than the previous candle's close price. But each candle's prices would close at higher levels.

Bearish Candlestick Patterns

The candlestick patterns that indicate a bearish bias for the market is called as Bearish candlestick patterns.

These patterns can be used for identifying good exit points for a trade, as well as for setting stop loss levels.

Following are some of the important bearish candlestick patterns:

- ☐ Bearish Engulfing

- ☐ Bearish Dark Cloud Cover

- ☐ Bearish Shooting star

- ☐ Hanging Man

- ☐ Bearish Belt Hold

- ☐ Bearish Harami/ Harami Cross

- ☐ Bearish Doji Star

- ☐ Bearish Abandoned Baby

- ☐ Bearish Evening Star

#1 Bearish Engulfing: Bearish Engulfing pattern indicates an upcoming top reversal and happens during an uptrend. It comprises of two candlesticks. The first candle would be a small white candle.

The second candle would be a long black candle which would completely engulf the body (but not necessarily the shadows) of the first day's white candle.

#2 Bearish Dark Cloud cover: Bearish Dark Cloud Cover is a top reversal pattern that takes place during a bull run. This pattern consists of two candlesticks. The first candle would be a white one.

The second candle would be a black candle which opens at a new high with a gap up and closes more than halfway into the body of first day's candle.

#3 Bearish Shooting star: Bearish Shooting star pattern indicates an upcoming trend reversal of the prevailing bull market. This pattern consists of two candlesticks. The first candle would be a white candle.

The second candle would be an inverted hammer with a small body and a long shadow at the top.

#4 Bearish Belt Hold: Bearish Belt Hold pattern is formed during a price uptrend and indicates an upcoming reversal of trend to bear market. This pattern consists of a single black candlestick. The candle would open at a high price for the day and would close at the low price of the day (or very near to it), resulting in a tall black candle.

#5 Bearish Harami/ Harami Cross: Bearish Harami, as well as Harami Cross, are bearish reversal patterns that comprise of two candlesticks.

In Bearish Harami Pattern, the first candle would be a tall white candle.

The second candle would be a black candle that would have a small body. This second candle would be completely within the range of the first candlestick's body.

In the case of Bearish Harami Cross pattern, there is just one minor difference – the second candlestick would be a doji.

#6 Bearish Doji Star: Bearish Doji Star is a top reversal pattern that is seen during a bullish uptrend. It consists of two candles. The first candle would be a long white candle. The second candle would open with an upward gap and its body would remain higher than that of the first candle's body. The second candle would close with the price almost the same as open price, resulting in a doji. The length of the shadow of the second candle would also be short.

#7 Bearish Abandoned Baby: Bearish Abandoned Baby is a rare bearish reversal candlestick pattern. It consists of three candles. The first candle would be a white candle.

The second candle would be a doji that would be formed by gapping upwards. The shadow of this doji would remain above the high of the first candle.

The third candle would be a black candle which would be formed gapped down below the second candle. The upper shadow of this third black candle would be below the low of the second (doji) candle.

#8 Bearish Evening Star: Bearish Evening Star candlestick pattern foretells an upcoming bearish reversal. It consists of three candlesticks.

The first candle would be a long white candle formed during a price uptrend.

The second candle would be a small white/ black candle that gaps up above the body of the first candle.

The third candle would be a tall black candle. The open price of this third candle would be below the second candle. The close price of the third candle would be at least mid-way of the body of the first candle.

Although there are few more candlestick patterns in existence, the above-mentioned candlesticks are the most vital ones.

Important Technical indicators for Penny Stocks

Before moving onto the advanced strategies for Buying as well as Exiting Penny Stocks, you must have a good understanding of the some of the important technical indicators of Penny Stocks. Here, you will be given a brief overview of the following– RSI, MACD, Stochastic, and Bollinger Bands.

RSI

RSI or Relative Strength Index indicates the momentum of a stock. This bound oscillator (of range 0 to 100) is used for identifying overbought and oversold levels of the security.

(Fig) RSI indicator

☐ When the value of RSI is **above** 70, it is considered as **overbought**.

☐ When the value of RSI is **below** 30, it is considered as **oversold.**

Full Stochastic Oscillator

Full Stochastic Oscillator, typically called as stochastics is a momentum indicator. It is used for identifying overbought and oversold levels of a security.

(Fig) Full Stochastic Oscillator

☐ When the value of Stochastics is **above** 80, it is considered as **overbought**.

☐ When the value of Stochastics is **below** 20, it is considered as **oversold.**

MACD

MACD or Moving Average Convergence Divergence is a simple as well as efficient momentum indicator that can be used for trend following as well. MACD consists of three parts – MACD line, Signal Line, and MACD Histogram.

(Fig) MACD Indicator

MACD Line is typically a black line. It is formed when the 12 day EMA of the closing price of security is subtracted from 26-day EMA of the closing price of the security. In short,

- ☐ MACD Line = (26-day EMA – 12 day EMA) of stock's closing price

Signal Line is typically red in color. It is the 9 day EMA of MACD Line. In short,

- ☐ Signal Line = 9-day EMA of MACD Line

MACD Histogram is formed by decreasing Signal Line from MACD Line

- ☐ MACD Histogram = MACD Signal Line – MACD Line

- ☐ MACD Histogram is **positive** when MACD Line crosses above Signal Line

- ☐ MACD Histogram is **negative** when MACD Line crosses below Signal Line

Bollinger Bands

Bollinger bands are volatility indicators. It comprises of an upper band, lower band, and middle band.

- ☐ Middle band is the 20 day SMA

The upper band is found by adding 20-day SMA with a 20-day standard deviation of price multiplied by 2.

- Upper band = 20 day SMA + (2 X 20 day standard deviation of price)

The lower band is found by subtracting the 20-day standard deviation of price multiplied by 2 from 20-day SMA.

- Lower band = 20-day SMA - (2 X 20-day standard deviation of price)

(Fig) Bollinger Bands

- If the price moves towards the top of Bollinger band, the prices are said to be high

- If the price moves towards the bottom of Bollinger band, the prices are said to be low

Chapter 3: Penny Stocks – Advanced Analysis

Importance of Tools and Resources for picking out Penny Stock winners

Out of the numerous Penny Stock available, identifying good ones by trial and error is simply not feasible. Not only is it time-consuming, it is also a highly exhausting and mind-numbing process.

This is where the mentality of a smart investor is different. He or she would make use of available tools and resources (like stock screeners) for picking out Penny Stocks that fits specific criteria.

Before we get into the details pertaining to Stock Screeners, below are the important tips for picking out companies that are Penny Stock winners and the red flags to look out for in order to identify the Penny Stock losers.

How to identify potential Penny Stock Winners?

A quick and easy way to identify a potential winner amongst Penny Stocks is to watch out for the following characteristics of the company:

#1 Valuation: In case the company has a low market cap when compared to its sales or book value, it indicates that the company has a good valuation. The stocks of such company

have a high probability of breaking out and giving lots of profit to the investor.

#2 *High Growth Rate:* Verify if the company is reporting high growth quarter on quarter. Even if the year on year growth doesn't seem exceptional, the company is a potential multi-bagger in case its quarter-to-quarter growth for previous two to three quarters are phenomenal.

#3 *Cash reserves:* Check out the cash reserves of the company before investing in its stocks. The rule of thumb is that companies with good cash reserves are highly likely to provide good returns.

How to avoid Penny Stock Losers – Major Red flags to look for

Below are some of the red flags to look out for in order to identify Penny Stock Losers. Avoid trading the stock of such companies as far as possible

#1 *Cash balance lower than $250,000:* When looking at the asset column of the company's balance sheet, if the cash balance is less than $250,000, it is best to avoid such companies.

#2 *Long term and Short term Debt:* Avoid the Penny Stocks that has a

☐ Short Term Debt higher than Cash balance.

☐ Long-term Debt higher than Zero.

#3 Signs of Pump and Dump scheme: It is best to be cautious about stocks that get aggressively promoted using press releases, insider information, newsletters, bulletin boards etc. Such actions indicate a probable pumping activity done by pump and dump schemes.

How to take advantage of Stock Screeners

There are numerous stock screeners available that can be used for picking out Penny Stock winners. Some of them are paid – like OptionsXpress while some others are free – like busystock or OTC market stock screeners. The functionalities available for these stock screeners also varies depending on the cost. Below is a guideline for using these stock screeners effectively.

1. Pick a price range for the stock you intend to trade or invest in. Then set the price filter to that range (say, under $1).

2. Adjust the volume filter to a higher setting in order to select stocks with high volume levels. Doing so will help you find stocks that have a good liquidity.

3. If interested, include any technical or fundamental analysis indicators as well in the filter criteria. This is optional.

4. Click on the search button to get a list of Penny Stocks that fulfill all your selected search criteria.

5. Among the resulting list of stocks, check for any alerts regarding scams, bankruptcy, or fraud. Eliminate those stocks from the list.

6. From the resultant list, apply the appropriate trading strategies (mentioned in the next chapter) in order to find the entry as well as exit criteria for the stock.

Thus, stock screeners can be effectively used for eliminating undesirable stocks while refining the search criteria for picking out Penny Stock winners.

Chapter 4: Advanced Strategies for Buying a Penny Stock

Various buying strategies can be used for Penny Stocks depending upon the prevailing trend of the stock.

Case 1: Advanced strategies for Stocks in Uptrend

This section contains advanced strategies for identifying the buy level for Penny Stocks that are in an uptrend. In case of a Penny Stock that in a strong uptrend, following two strategies can be used to take a long position at appropriate times

☐ Advanced buying strategy using moving averages cross over and Stochastics

☐ Advanced strategy using multi-time frames and RSI

#1: Advanced buying strategy using moving averages cross over and Stochastics

Advanced buying strategy using moving averages cross over and Stochastics is based on the combination of two moving averages and the stochastics on the weekly chart of the Penny Stock. The basic concept is to buy the Penny Stock on the breakout after a long period of consolidation.

Trading Strategy: The trading strategy involves the crossover of two moving averages. Among the two moving averages, one should be of shorter duration and the other of a longer duration. The two moving averages that are best suited for this strategy are the 20-week moving average and the 50-week moving average. These two moving averages would then be used in conjunction with the stochastic indicator to get the entry signal.

Most Penny Stocks consolidate for a long period of time before breaking out of a range and starting the uptrend. The moving averages help in entering the stock when the momentum starts building up.

Identifying Uptrend: Once the price starts to trade above the moving averages and the shorter moving average crosses above the longer moving average, the stock is said to be in an uptrend.

Entry Criteria: The entry signal for the strategy is as follows

- ☐ The price starts to trade above both the moving averages.

- ☐ The shorter moving average crosses above the longer moving average.

- ☐ Stochastic is in the oversold region.

This is best explained using an example.

Example: Following is the chart of a Penny Stock Independence Energy Stock (IDNG). According to the strategy, the entry signal for going long on this Penny Stock would be when

- ☐ IDNG starts trading above the two moving averages

- ☐ The 20 day WMA crosses the 50 WMA.

☐   Stochastic is oversold.

The entry signal is marked on the chart below.

(Fig) Strategy using Moving Averages cross over and Stochastics

Re-entry during Correction: For traders who missed out on buying the stock on the initial buy signal, they can look to enter the stock on corrections. Such re-entry points are also marked on the chart.

Ideally, the re-entry should be when the stock corrects to the space between the two moving averages. A bullish reversal candle forming in the space between the moving averages is an ideal point to enter the stock after a correction.

#2: Advanced buying strategy using multi-time frames and RSI.

Advanced buying strategy using multi-time frames and RSI involves analyzing the stock on the daily and the weekly time frame and checking if the RSI levels indicate a favorable entry setup. Analyzing the stock using both daily as well as weekly time frames would provide an added margin of safety and help in fine tuning the entry.

Trading Strategy: First, the stock would be analyzed on the weekly chart. It should fulfill a specific set of criteria on the weekly chart. Then, the stock would be analyzed on the daily charts. Once it fulfills a specific set of conditions on the daily chart as well, entry can be made for the stock as long as the RSI is in the specific range of values.

Entry Criteria – Analyzing Weekly Chart: Following are the conditions to be fulfilled on the weekly chart.

- ☐ The stock should be in an **uptrend** on the weekly chart. This means that the stock should make higher highs and higher lows on the weekly chart.

- ☐ The stock should be trading above the **30-day** moving average.

- ☐ The **RSI** should be either

   - o In the oversold region – ie, 20 or below

   - o Above 20 and moving in an upwards direction; but not yet reached the overbought region (i.e. above 80)

☐ High volume **bearish reversal candles** (hanging man, doji, evening star etc.) should **not** be formed on the weekly chart.

Once the above criteria are met on the weekly charts, the stock should then be analyzed on the daily chart to get an entry point.

Entry Criteria – Analyzing Daily Chart: Once the weekly uptrend is established, following conditions in the daily chart can be used for taking a long position

☐ The stock corrects and takes **support** at the **trend line**. Ideally, the stock should form a bullish reversal candle (hammer, morning star etc.) near the trend line.

☐ The **RSI** should be either

o In the oversold region i.e. 20 or below

o Above 20 and moving in an upwards direction; but not yet reached the overbought region (i.e. above 80)

The basic premise is to buy on pullbacks or corrections on the daily chart while the main trend on the weekly chart remains intact.

This strategy is best explained with an example.

Example: Following is the chart of a Penny Stock Kraig Biocraft Laboratories Inc (KBLB). According to the strategy, an entry signal is generated in the weekly chart for going long on this Penny Stock due to the following reasons.

☐ On the weekly chart of KBLB, the stock has been making higher highs and higher lows indicating that the stock is in an uptrend.

☐ The RSI is 60 which is below the overbought area, so there is more room for the uptrend to continue.

☐ KBLB is trading above 30-day SMA.

(Fig) Entry on weekly charts: Multi-time frames and RSI strategy

Next, we need to move on to the daily chart of KBLB to get a suitable entry point.

As per the daily chart of KBLB, an entry signal is generated for the stock due to the following reasons.

- The stock has corrected back to the trend line.

- A bullish reversal candle (hammer), has formed in this area which means that the immediate downtrend is over and the stock has taken support in this region.

- The RSI is above 20 and moving up.

(Fig) Entry on daily charts: Multi-time frames and RSI strategy

So the conditions are satisfied on the daily chart as well and hence, the buy signal is generated. This is marked on the chart.

The past buy signal is also marked on the chart.

Case 2: Advanced strategies for stocks that breakout from a range

The next two strategies can be used when a Penny Stock breaks out of a range. Most Penny Stock consolidates for a long time before making a big up move. The period of consolidation can last from a few weeks to a few months. It is important to make an entry only after the breakout is validated to avoid false breakouts.

Following are the strategies for trading stocks that breakout from a range:

- ☐ Advanced buying strategy using Bollinger bands and MACD lines

- ☐ Advanced buying strategy using price action and volume

#3: Advanced buying strategy using Bollinger bands and MACD lines

Advanced buying strategy using Bollinger bands and MACD lines makes use of MACD lines as well as Bollinger Bands to determine the entry point of the trade. This strategy is highly useful for buying Penny Stock just before they break out of a narrow range.

Settings: The settings of Bollinger bands and MACD to be used for this strategy is their default settings.

Trading Strategy: First, scan for stocks that have a Bollinger squeeze. The scan is done either manually by checking each stock individually or by making use of the scan feature that some trading platforms provide

Note: Bollinger squeeze is said to occur when the volatility is low and the Bollinger band narrows.

In most cases, a big move follows after a period of low volatility. So, after identifying the stock that has a Bollinger squeeze, you must wait for the stock to breakout of the squeeze or in other words, wait for the Bollinger band to expand.

Entry Criteria: The buy signal is generated when the following conditions are satisfied.

- ☐ When the stock breaks out of the squeeze

- ☐ When the fast moving MACD line crosses the slow moving line.

This is best explained with the help of an example.

Example: Following is the chart of a Penny Stock Amarin Corp PLC ADS (AMRN). As you can see from the chart, the stock was in a Bollinger squeeze initially. This period of Bollinger Squeeze is marked on the chart.

This Bollinger Squeeze indicates a period of low volatility. During this period of low volatility, the stock should be kept on the radar, but no action should be taken.

Following is the entry criteria for the trade.

- Once the stock breaks out of the squeeze and the band expands a buy signal is generated. This is marked on the chart below.

- In order to confirm the strength of the breakout, the MACD lines should crossover as well.

Once these two criteria are met, an entry can be made into the stock. As seen from the chart, a big up move followed the period of low volatility or the Bollinger squeeze.

(Fig) Strategy using Bollinger Bands and MACD Lines

In a nutshell, this strategy can be summarized as

- Scan for stocks that have Bollinger squeeze and keep them on the watch list

- Wait for the stock to break out of the squeeze and for the band to expand.

☐ Take a long position when the MACD lines crossover.

#4: Advanced buying strategy using price action and volume

Advanced buying strategy using price action and volume is based on the price action and the corresponding volume of a Penny Stock. As mentioned earlier, most Penny Stocks undergo a period of consolidation before a breakout or an uptrend. But first, it is important to understand a few basic concepts regarding price action before we delve deeper into this strategy.

A prerequisite for understanding this strategy would be a basic comprehension about candlesticks. A long (wide), green (white) candle usually indicates that a strong up move has happened. But it is important to use this in conjunction with volume to get a bigger picture.

☐ A long candle with high volume indicates that the up move is backed by strong hands or smart money, whereas

☐ A long candle with low volume might not necessarily indicate that the buying was by smart money.

Note: The term **smart money** refers to strong financial institutions like banks, mutual funds etc., or foreign investors. It is important to remain on the same side as the smart money to raises your odds of a profitable trade. So, identifying the price action is very important.

Similarly, a narrow green (white) candle with a high volume might not be a good sign because it indicates that the smart money was distributing or selling the stock.

Trading strategy: According to this strategy, first identify Penny Stocks that are consolidating or in a range. In most cases, the Penny Stocks would be consolidating inside a channel. Then go for long positions when breakout happens supported with huge volume surge.

Entry Criteria: The entry signal for this strategy would be triggered when the stock breaks out the channel or range on high volumes. The term high volumes imply volumes that are at least 5 times the normal volume levels of the previous 6 months.

This is best explained with an example.

Example: Following is the chart of a Penny Stock Northern Dynasty Minerals Limited (NDK). As you can see from the chart, NAK was consolidating inside a channel for several weeks before it finally broke out of the channel.

(Fig) Strategy using Price action and Volume

Following are the two entry points for taking long positions.

☐ At the lower end of the channel whenever there is a long legged candle. This usually indicates a selling climax before a big up move begins. Selling climax is nothing but the shaking out of weaker hands by the smart money. This is the entry point # 1 marked on the chart

☐ When the price breaks out of the channel on high volumes. This is marked as entry point # 2 on the chart.

The second entry point is safer because the entry is made only after the breakout occurs from the range. But on the downside, it would be less profitable than the trades done at entry point # 1.

Case 3: Advanced strategy for Pre- Spike Identification

This section is probably the most anticipated one. Here, you will be learning about trading strategies that can be used to identify Penny Stock winners pre-spike. After all, the early bird gets the worm et all.

Following are the advanced strategies:

☐ Advanced buying strategy using MACD histogram positive divergence

☐ Advanced buying strategy using bullish candlestick patterns

#5: Advanced buying strategy using MACD histogram positive divergence

Advanced buying strategy using MACD histogram positive divergence is useful for buying beaten down Penny Stocks. This strategy helps in identifying stocks which have a positive divergence in MACD histogram and price. Such divergence indicates that the down momentum of the stock is weakening and a reversal is around the corner.

A prerequisite for understanding this strategy would be a basic comprehension about MACD histogram and divergence.

MACD Histogram: Like mentioned earlier, MACD Histogram is the difference between the fast moving MACD line and the signal line. This difference is then plotted to get a histogram. The MACD histogram is very useful in finding divergences.

Divergence: Although there are several different types of divergences, the divergence referenced here is the price and the MACD divergence.

So what exactly is a divergence? A positive divergence occurs when

☐ The price makes a lower low but

☐ The indicator (MACD histogram in this case), makes a higher low.

Trading Strategy: First, identify the stocks that are currently at a beaten down level, but shows a positive divergence between MACD Histogram and price. Such a positive divergence indicates that even though the price was driven lower to make a lower low, the indicator did not follow suit. This essentially means that the downward momentum is reducing and a possible reversal is around the corner for the stock.

Entry Criteria: The entry should be made as soon as the MACD histogram starts moving up. This means that the entry point would be the next candle after the upmove starts for MACD Histogram.

This is best explained with an example.

Example: Following is the chart of a Penny Stock Amarin Corp PLC ADS (AMRN). This can be used to understand the price and MACD divergence as well as when an entry signal is generated.

The stock of was on a down trend making lower lows and lower highs. In the month of February, the stock made a lower low, but the MACD histogram made a higher low. This indicated that the selling pressure was reducing and the stock was on the brink of a possible reversal.

The buy signal for this setup would be when the MACD histogram makes a shorter bar or starts moving up. This is marked on the chart below. As can be seen from the chart, the stock rallied from there on after.

(Fig) Strategy using MACD Histogram - Price positive divergence

This method is quite useful in identifying beaten down Penny Stocks but it's important to understand that there is no guarantee that this method would work all the time. After all technical analysis just raises our odds of success. So it is important to keep a Stop loss. The ideal stop loss would be a few cents below the last pivot low.

#6: Advanced buying strategy using bullish candlestick patterns

Bullish candlestick patterns indicate that the demand is greater than the supply. When the demand is greater than the supply, only longs should be taken. There are several bullish candlestick patterns, and some of the important ones have been discussed earlier in the book.

Trading Strategy: First, identify the stocks which have bullish candlestick patterns being formed. Then use these bullish candlestick patterns in conjunction with an indicator like RSI or Stochastic to get a more accurate buy signal.

In order to get a more accurate and reliable buy signal, it is better to use the weekly chart while using this strategy.

Let us understand this strategy using two bullish candlestick patterns: the hammer and the bullish inside bar (Bullish Harami).

Hammer: The hammer is usually formed at the end of a downtrend. Since it has a long wick, it indicates that even though the stock went down over the week, there was buying pressure causing the stock to bounce back towards the end of the week. This is a strong bullish candlestick.

Bullish Harami: The bullish inside bar (or Bullish Harami) is usually formed after a big black (bearish) candle i.e. after a week where the stock moved down drastically.

The candle formed after the black candle is called an inside bar if its entire range remains within the range of the previous candle. Some people also call it an inside bar even if just the body of the candle remains within the range of the previous week's candle.

The candle referred here is a weekly candle, as the strategy involves the use of a weekly time frame. (Inside bar can form in any time frame.)

Entry Criteria - Hammer: The entry can be made when

- ☐ The Hammer pattern is formed on the weekly chart, and

- ☐ RSI is in the oversold region.

- ☐ RSI can also be slightly above the oversold region and moving up

This is best explained with an example.

Example: In the below chart of FTR, the stock was in a downtrend making lower highs and lower lows. On the week of Jan 2016, the stock made a hammer pattern.

This indicated that the demand was increasing, probably because the buyers felt that the stock was now trading at a fair value. At the same time, RSI was in the oversold region, further confirming the buy signal.

(Fig) Hammer and RSI

The stop loss for the trade would be a few pips below the low of the hammer. As we can see from the chart, the stock rallied from there on in.

Entry Criteria – Bullish Harami: The entry can be made when

☐ The Inside Bar pattern is formed on the weekly chart, and

- RSI is in the oversold region.

- RSI can also be slightly above the oversold region and moving up

This is best explained with an example.

Example: In the chart of MNKD the stock has been on a downtrend. On the week of January 2016, the stock formed a big black candle. In the week that followed, the stock formed an inside bar as can be seen from the chart.

This indicated that the selling pressure has reduced. The buyers were now back, probably because they felt that the stock has reached a region of fair value now.

The RSI was also in the oversold region, thus generating a buy signal.

(Fig) Bullish Harami and RSI

Alternate Trading Strategy using Bullish Candlestick Patterns:

Another strategy to use the bullish candlesticks for an entry point is to wait for a bullish reversal candlestick in important **support areas**. Once the bullish candle is formed in the support area, it validates the strength of the support area. These areas are good **entry points**.

This again can be used in conjunction with RSI to identify an even better entry point. Ideally,

☐ The RSI should be in the oversold region.

☐ RSI can also be slightly above the oversold region and moving up.

Chapter 5: Advanced Strategies for Exiting a Penny Stock

Exiting a trade is equally important as entering a trade. There are mainly three reasons for it.

- ☐ The profits become real only once the trade is completed.

- ☐ Exiting at the correct point will prevent losing all the profits made till then.

- ☐ In order to short sell a Penny Stock, although this is not advised.

Hence, it is vital that you understand the selling strategies for exiting Penny Stocks. It is important to book profits on the first sign of weakness especially in Penny Stocks.

What is an Exit strategy? Exit strategies are basically combinations of patterns and indicators that help in identifying the possible tops from where the market could correct drastically.

Essentially, exit strategies help in identifying weakness or selling pressure, right when it starts.

Following are some important selling strategies for Penny Stocks that would help in exiting from a Penny Stock before it starts going down.

- ☐ Advanced Exit Strategy based on negative MACD divergence

☐ Advanced Exit Strategy based on Moving Averages crossover

☐ Advanced Exit Strategy based on Trendline Breakdown

☐ Advanced Exit Strategy based on RSI negative divergence

☐ Advanced Exit Strategy based on bearish candlestick patterns

#1 Advanced Exit Strategy based on negative MACD divergence

A Divergence occurs when the price and the indicator start behaving differently. A negative divergence occurs when the price makes higher highs but the indicator makes lower highs. This basically indicates that even the stock has been moving higher, the momentum has been weakening. This indicates that a possible bearish reversal is around the corner.

Trading Strategy: First, check for any negative divergence between MACD and Price. In case there is an MACD negative divergence,

☐ The price would make a higher high but

☐ Either the MACD lines or MACD histogram makes a lower high.

Exit Criteria: The exit should be made as soon as the MACD histogram starts moving down. This means that the exit point would be

- The next candle after the down move starts for MACD Histogram Or,

- MACD forms a shorter histogram bar

This is best explained with an example.

Example: In the chart of NETE, the price has been moving up as shown in the chart. But this move was not supported by the MACD as it was making lower highs.

So once this setup has been identified, the exit signal would be on the candlestick where the MACD forms a shorter histogram bar. These have been marked on the chart.

(Fig) MACD – Price negative divergence Exit Strategy

As seen from the chart, the stock corrected drastically after that.

#2 Advanced Exit Strategy based on RSI negative divergence

This strategy is similar to the MACD divergence. The only difference is that RSI is used instead of MACD.

The divergence occurs when the price makes a higher high and the RSI makes a lower high, indicating that the momentum is reducing.

Example: In the chart of NETE, the price made a higher high in April – May 2016, but the RSI made a lower high at the same time.

Once the pattern is identified, the exit signal is triggered when the stock forms a bearish reversal candle. All these have been marked on the chart below.

(Fig) RSI – Price negative divergence Exit Strategy

#3 Advanced Exit Strategy based on Moving Averages crossover

Moving averages can be used to determine if the stock is losing momentum. In case the stock starts to lose momentum, exiting the stock can be considered.

Typically, the 200-day moving average is used to decide the trend of a stock. It is considered bullish if the stock is trading above the 200-day moving average and bearish if it is trading below it.

There are two trading strategies based on how risk averse you are with respect to trading Penny Stocks.

Trading Strategy 1: After an uptrend, if the stock corrects and closes below the 200-day moving average, then it indicates that the uptrend is over and exiting the stock right then would be a good option.

Trading Strategy 2: However, if the stock were to close below the 200-day moving average, it would have already corrected to a good extent. Hence, your exit would become a tad late. For traders who want to make a faster exit, pick the exit signal based on the combination of 20-day and 50-day moving average.

Exit Criteria for Trading Strategy 2: The exit signal is triggered when

- ☐ The price closes below the 20-day moving average

- ☐ The 20-day moving average crosses below the 50-day moving average

This indicates a short-term weakness and an exit can be planned.

This is best explained using an example.

Example: The stock COSI was in a steady uptrend making higher highs and higher lows. On last week of April, the stock closed below its 20-day moving average and soon after the 20-day moving average crossed below the 50-day moving average, generating an exit signal.

(Fig)   Exit Strategy using moving averages crossover

As can be seen from the chart, the stock corrected substantially after that.

Any combination of moving averages can be used for this strategy. It is important to back test and see which combination works well in a particular market for a particular stock. A few of the other common combinations are 10 and 30, 15 and 40 and 50 and 200.

#4 Advanced Exit Strategy based on Trendline Breakdown

When a stock is in an uptrend, it usually makes a series of well-defined higher lows or pivot lows.

*A **pivot low*** is the last low made before the stock makes a new high. These pivot lows or higher lows can be joined to form a **trend line**.

In most cases as long as the trend is up, the stock respects the trend line. In other words, when the stock corrects and reaches the trend line, it is considered to be of fair value and demand exists. Thus, the stock takes support at the trend line. So as long as the stock holds this trend line it can be said to be in an uptrend.

Trading Strategy: First, identify the stocks in an uptrend with a clear defined trend line. Once the stock goes below the trend line, it shows that the trend is weakening. Make the exit when the exit signal is triggered.

Exit Criteria: Following are the conditions for the exit.

☐ When the stock goes below trend line

☐ If the stock goes below the previous pivot low.

This would indicate that the uptrend has indeed ended.

This is best explained with an example.

Example: In the chart of FTR, the stock was in a strong uptrend making higher highs and higher lows. A trend line has been drawn on the chart by joining all the pivot lows.

In the month of June 2015, the stock broke down from the trend line. Traders who are risk averse can even consider exiting the stock at this point (Exit #1).

But it is better to wait for the stock to go below the previous pivot low (Exit #2) to make sure that the trend has indeed ended.

(Fig) Exit Strategy based on trend line breakdown

As seen from the chart, a few days later, the stock goes below the previous pivot low, indicating that the trend is over.

It is better to exit the stock at this point as a period of the uptrend is usually followed either by sideways movement or a down trend.

#5 Advanced Exit Strategy based on bearish candlestick patterns

Candlesticks patterns give a good indication of the balance between supply and demand. Bullish candlestick patterns are those which indicate that the demand is greater than the supply. Conversely, bearish reversal candles indicate that the supply is greater than the demand. For now, only in the bearish reversal candles would be discussed as the focus is on exit strategies.

Trading Strategy: First, identify the stocks which have **bearish** candlestick patterns being formed. Note that candlesticks should not be used as a standalone tool for exiting a stock. Hence, these bearish candlestick patterns should be used in conjunction with an indicator like **stochastics**.

It is better to use these candlestick patterns on the weekly chart for determining the exit point from a Penny Stock. Various bearish candlestick patterns have been discussed earlier in this book. Here, the focus is given a bearish pattern – bearish engulfing with relevant examples.

Exit Criteria – Bearish Engulfing: The exit can be made when

   ☐ The Bearish Engulfing pattern is formed on the weekly chart, and

   ☐ Stochastic is in the overbought region.

   ☐ RSI can also be slightly above the overbought region and moving down

This is best explained with an example.

Example: In the chart below of GERN the stock was on an uptrend, making higher highs and higher lows. The stock formed a bearish engulfing with good volumes in December 2015.

Bearish engulfing is a major reversal candle and it indicates that the supply is getting stronger. The bearish engulfing candle completely covered the range of the previous candle, indicating strong supply.

(Fig) Bearish Engulfing and Stochastic

At the same time, Stochastic was in the overbought zone. This further confirms the weakness and an exit signal is generated. The stock went down after the exit signal was generated

Chapter 6: Money Management

Successful investing as well as trading in Penny Stocks require clear and defined money management rules and tips. They help in reigning in the losses while maximizing the profits. This chapter on money management deals precisely with this concept. For ease of understanding, it is divided into two sections

□ Money management for Penny Stocks trading

□ Money management for Penny Stocks investment

Money management for Penny Stocks trading

Trading can yield both profits as well as losses. But many times, traders are unsure about when to book the profits. They keep on holding the stock in anticipation that the trade would turn more profitable, and may eventually have to sell at a loss.

Conversely, many traders hold onto losing trades in the anticipation and hope that the tide will turn and the trade would become profitable. This could result in massive losses.

The following section contains guidelines and tips on when to book profits as well as when to take losses. These tips can be used in conjunction with the various exit strategies mentioned in the earlier chapter.

#1 When to book profits?

For trades which are at a profit, the ideal position to exit is in the following cases

- [ ] When the price of the stock is significantly higher than the original buy price, look into booking at least half of the purchased quantity. This strategy also makes the holding of the remaining stocks less risky.

- [ ] In case there is any breaking news that seems unfavorable to the company whose stocks that you are holding, exit the stock immediately and book profits.

- [ ] When the stocks start trading at a high price, but with a low volume, it shows signs of weakening of stock. Hence, it is best to book profits and exit the trade.

#2 When to take losses?

Following are tips to exit trades which are at a loss

- [ ] When the stop loss level is reached – Many times, traders hold onto stock even when it reaches the stock's planned stop loss, leading to additional losses. It is always best to simply exit the trade at planned stop loss. This helps in maintaining the trading discipline as well.

- [ ] In case the trade was taken based on the rumors pertaining to specific upcoming developments of the company, check the price action after the said event comes to fruition. If the stock price is not moving well despite the development, it is best to ditch the stock even at a loss.

☐ If there is a huge increase in the trading volume without much changes happening in the price, it is a **bad** sign. It signifies a potential sell-off from investors. Hence, it is best to exit the trade when such a phenomenon is observed, even if you have to book losses.

Money management for Penny Stocks investment

Unlike trading, investment requires long-term planning. Following are two important strategies for Penny Stock investment:

☐ Position Sizing

☐ Dollar cost averaging

Importance of Dollar Cost Averaging

One of the most common mistakes done by both novice Penny Stock investors and veterans alike is to buy the entire quantity of stocks (that is intended to be purchased) on a single day itself. The stock market is too fluid, as its direction changes based on even a rumor or breaking news. Due to this, you would not be able to plan the exact moment to invest in a stock in such a manner that it would maximize your profit.

This is best explained with an example. Assume that you invested in 2000 stocks of company XYZ on Monday costing you $2000 in total.

Case1: On Tuesday, the CEO of the company resigns due to some accounting scandal. The market reacts to the news and the stock corrects from $1 to $0.65. Had you waited for a day before making the investment, you could have bought 2000 stocks of the company for $1300, effectively saving you $700.

Case 2: Conversely, assume that a product of the company XYZ won a patent on Tuesday, causing its stock price to rise to $1.30 from the original $1. Had you waited for another day to invest, you would have had to shell out $2600, which is $600 more than the previous day!

As you can see, it is difficult to precisely time when the investment should be made. Depending on the news of the day, the price of the stock could either increase or decrease. This is where the Dollar Cost Averaging (or Pound Cost Averaging) strategy gains importance.

What is Dollar Cost Averaging? In Dollar cost averaging strategy, the stock is bought using a fixed sum of money on a specific schedule (say, every 3 months or 6 months) regardless of the stock's price. Typically, the number of stocks purchased are low when the stock price is high, while a higher number of stocks are bought when the stock price is lower.

Why Dollar Cost Averaging?

    ☐ By using this strategy, the average price of the stock would be lower in comparison to the bulk purchase.

- [ ] It also lowers the probability of risking a huge amount at a wrong time.

- [ ] The recommended wait period between two purchases is six months to a year.

- [ ] Although it might result in a higher broker commission, the overall benefit surpasses the higher broker cost.

Uses of Dollar Cost Averaging: Dollar Cost Averaging strategy is highly useful in protecting your investment against

- [ ] The market's downside risk as well as

- [ ] Market fluctuations.

Risk: This strategy does not protect the money in case the stock you had invested in is in a free fall. This can be avoided to an extent by researching the stock thoroughly (including the technical as well as fundamental analysis) before doing the investment.

Who should use this strategy? This strategy is ideal for Penny Stock investors who are

- [ ] Risk averse

- [ ] Looking for long term investment

- [ ] Wants to invest in a stock which is historically volatile in its price.

- [ ] Looking into investing in a market which is in a temporary downtrend.

Importance of Position sizing

Another important strategy pertaining to Penny Stock investing is Position Sizing. This is one of the most misunderstood, albeit powerful investing strategy. It is based on purely mathematical calculations and help in controlling risks while providing maximum profits.

What is position sizing? The concept of position sizing is to basically set a percentage limit or dollar limit of the individual's portfolio for purchasing stocks. This is best explained using hypothetical portfolio and stock example.

Assume that an individual's total portfolio is worth $100,000

☐ If $5000 worth of stock 'ABC' is present in the portfolio, it means that ABC has a position size of 5%.

☐ On the other hand, if $15,000 worth of stock 'LMN' is present in the portfolio, it has a position size of 15%.

The basic idea of position sizing strategy is to ***limit*** the percentage of your account in a single position. For instance, you can set the ***limit as 4%***.

In that case, in the $100,000 portfolio, no stock should be present which is worth more than 4% of the total value (or $4000).

Why position sizing?

☐ Prevents catastrophic losses to the portfolio

☐ Diversifies portfolio

☐ Safeguards portfolio against market crashes to an extent

Risk: This downside of this strategy is that it limits the profits. For example, assume that the stock 'PQR' of your portfolio had a huge move upwards. (say, from $1 to $2) Had you invested in this stock for say, around 90% of the portfolio, your portfolio would have gained huge profits. But since the percentage value of the stock in the portfolio is limited to just 5%, the profits gained are also limited.

Who should use this strategy? This strategy is ideal for Penny Stock investors

☐ Who have a large portfolio

☐ Who wants to avoid substantial losses to their portfolio

Note: The concept of position sizing can also be used in case of Penny Stock Trading. The rule of thumb here is that more than 1% of the trading capital should not be risked in a single trade. For example, if your trading account is for $500, you should not risk more than $5 on a trade.

Bonus Chapter: Secrets for Successful Penny Stock Trading

In order to become a successful Penny Stock Trader, you would need experience as well as education in equal measures. Educating yourself is an easier process, as you can simply read books or attend seminars. Experience, however, is a tricky thing, as it is not always written about in stock trading books.

In this bonus section, I will be disclosing some of my rules for trading Penny Stocks that has helped me maximize profits over the years.

1. Always have an exit plan in mind. Cut the losses and exit from trades if the trade doesn't go as planned. Remember that your wins from successful trades would quickly cover these small losses.

2. Keep a diary of your successful and not-so-successful trades. This will help you find out which trading style suits you the best, giving you maximum profits. Eventually, a trading framework can be built, and can be fine-tuned every now and then.

3. Avoid Penny Stocks that have a very low liquidity. Chances are, you will be stuck with those and unable to exit them as there are no buyers! Instead, pick the stocks that have high liquidity.

4. Trading based on gut instinct would work – around 10% of the time. The remaining 90% would cost you heavily! So, for consistent and steady profits, stick with your trading framework. Trust the numbers – they don't lie!

5. It is okay to wait it out if you do not find a good setup for entering trades. Desperation to trade just leads to losses.

6. The ideal amount of money to set aside for Penny Stock trading? $2000. Anything less would just lead to eating away your money before you even make profits.

7. Irrespective of the market conditions or direction, it is possible to make money as long as you have a good understanding of the basics.

8. The saying – don't put all your eggs in a single basket holds true for Penny Stocks as well. Never invest all your money into a single stock.

9. Always be proactive in finding out any breaking news, product launches, or mergers. Sometimes, google alerts and Facebook discussions might shed light on new developments when analysts and news agencies cannot.

Conclusion

Thank you again for downloading this book!

I hope this book was able to help you to understand the advanced concepts, advanced analysis and advanced strategies for picking out Penny Stock winners.

The next step is to apply the strategies and techniques mentioned in the book in real life for becoming a successful professional trader in Penny Stocks.

Finally, if you enjoyed this book, then I'd like to ask you for a favor, would you be kind enough to leave a review for this book on Amazon? It'd be greatly appreciated!

Click here to leave a review for this book on Amazon!

Thank you and good luck!

Made in United States
Orlando, FL
24 November 2021